Same River, Different Water

A Veteran's Journey from Vietnam to Việt Nam

Douglas Young

Photo preceding page:

The Perfume River, west of the city of Huế. Photo taken from atop Vọng Cảnh, a hill where young lovers now meet, and which was once used to guard the western approaches to the city during the war.

Photo on cover:

The Perfume River in the city of Huế at night, with traditional sampans in the water, but looking at modern buildings on the far shore.

ISBN-10: 1467906921
EAN-13: 9781467906920

Dedication

To my life partner, fellow veteran of the war in Vietnam, and a person who loves present day Việt Nam with the same passion as me—my wife Cindy. This book is as much about her as it is about me. We met in 1969, she a member of the U.S. Army Nurse Corps, and me an Infantry Captain.

Việt Nam became so much for us. We shared the adventure of living and working in the beautiful city of Huế in 2005–06 and have made many trips back since.

Cindy is the woman who lets me smoke cigars inside her house, who never complains when I buy another photography toy, who loves a bowl of *phở* as much as I do, and who does more than just tolerate my idio-syncrasies—she nudges them on.

Thank you for being the love of my life.

Anh yeu em.

Acknowledgments

I consider Mr. Phan Cu to be my best friend. Notice he is not my "best friend in Việt Nam." He is my best friend. Cu is one of the kindest gentlemen I have ever known. He gives to the poor, photographs weddings for couples who cannot afford to pay him, and generously helps foreign charitable groups operating in central Việt Nam. If it weren't for the fact that he is not particularly religious, he might be described as a "good Christian man." Cu and I spent many a happy hour taking photographs together. Though I had bought my first serious camera in Vietnam in 1969, it was Cu who inspired me to pick one up again four decades later. Thank you for putting a camera back in my hand, my friend.

I'm uncertain whether to blame or thank James Sullivan, the author of *Over the Moat: Love Among the Ruins of Imperial Việt Nam,* in which he chronicles meeting and courting his wife Thuy in Huế in 1992. James was fascinated by the fact that my wife and I were both veterans of the war yet chose to live and work in Việt Nam. James promised to edit my work if only I would write the story. If James had not prodded me, this book would not have happened. If James had not edited it, it would have been a very bad book.

Bill Paquette was the very first fellow veteran I contacted after the war—and that happened many years after Bill was seriously wounded in 1967. Though nice to find him again, it was even better to find a new friend. Jim "Tree" Machin also served with me during the war. In the late 1990s, Jim got me interested in the experiences we combat veterans had as members of Company C, 2nd Battalion, 5th Cavalry Regiment, 1st Cavalry Division. He organized numerous reunions for the many men who served in that unit from 1965 to 1972. If Jim hadn't first spurred my interest in thinking about Vietnam, I might never have returned to Việt Nam.

To the soldiers of Company B, 3rd Battalion 7th Infantry, 199th Light Infantry Brigade, and the troopers of Company C, 2nd Battalion 5th Cavalry, 1st Cavalry Division (Airmobile): You guys have absolutely no idea what a privilege it was to serve with you. Damn—we were good, weren't we?

And to the many others who offered ideas and encouragement or are an essential part of this book: Martha Young Stanley, Jeff Wilhoit, Phan Thuy Trang, Le Bao Tuan, Hoàng Thanh, Dr. William Hamilton, LaRelle and Robert Catherman, Julie Lopez (then Julie Louis), Thuy Sullivan, Ngo Ái Nhân, Lê Trung Kiên,

Marc and Kami Gavilanez, Chuck and Joette Ward, Ken and Heather Kimball, Russell and Patty Young, Larry Nyland Jr., Carol and Mick De Hart, Edwina Garza, Dr. Thomas Murray, Dương Lâm Anh, Keith and Misty Young, Leigh Fairbank, Nguyễn Huyen Nhi, Sandy Harrison, Ken Gardiner, John Orr, Hā Thuy Trâm, the late Father Bob Sutherland, Jerry "Doc" Watson, Doug Hendrixson, Mike Hayes, JB and Pat Townsend, the late Karen Young Fyke, Don Jensen, Nancy Farnum, Dr. Jason Stewart, Rev. Peter Galbraith, Gabe Hernandez, and Barbara Crookshank.

Writing about Việt Nam is akin to writing about digital technology—as soon as you publish, the information is obsolete. Việt Nam is changing so fast that what I first observed in 2002 on our first return trip became laughably out of date by 2011. One example is the Internet. In 2002, even the best hotels had no Wi-Fi; they had only a "business office" where guests could access their e-mail using a poor 14.4 dial-up connection. Every city block had multiple Internet cafés. By 2011, broadband DSL connections are found in small villages. Internet cafés are getting harder to find, as more people have computers at home. Incredibly, 95 percent of the children born since 1990 are online.

About Vietnamese names: they are placed in the reverse order of Western names, meaning the family names are first, followed by the middle name, and the given name is last. If I were Vietnamese, my name would be Young Alan Douglas. Additionally, unlike us, the Vietnamese use their given name in formal situations. To my Vietnamese students, I was Mr. Doug, not Mr. Young. Most Vietnamese change their name order to the Western style when they come to America. When Trang came to the United States to earn her Master's degree, she switched her name to Trang Phan. While working as a university lecturer, her students called her Miss Phan.

Doug Young
Mc Allen, Texas
April, 2012

We think you ought to know, dear brothers and sisters, about the trouble we went through in... Asia. We were crushed and overwhelmed beyond our ability to endure, and we thought we would never live through it. In fact, we expected to die. But as a result, we stopped relying on ourselves and learned to rely only on God, who raises the dead. And he did rescue us from mortal danger, and he will rescue us again. We have placed our confidence in him, and he will continue to rescue us.

2 Corinthians 1:8–10
(New Living Translation)

Contents

In the Beginning...

a Prologue

A mericans of a certain age are very familiar with Vietnam. In the 1960s, they saw it on their television sets every night. Many of them spent a year (or more) there—and just about everybody was related to or had a good friend who served there.

And many Americans of that certain age think they know a lot about the country.

An artist once told me that if I wanted to spur my mind and see things I had never seen before, I should stand with my feet apart, and then bend over from the waist until I was looking between my knees.

When I did, everything looked different—familiar objects took a little while to recognize because they were now upside down.

Going back to Việt Nam is like that for a veteran—the familiar is now very different. This book is about my bending over at the waist and looking between my knees—an unexpected way to see Vietnam from a very different perspective.

Sitting beside a swiftly moving river, dip your toe in the water, and then take it out. Five minutes later, dip the same toe in the water. Yes, the river's name is the same, but the water you touched before has gone downstream—your toe is now touching new water. The ancient Greek philosopher Heraclitus said, "No man ever steps in the same river twice." This book is about stepping in the new water in the river.

I use two different spellings of the name of the country in this book. The American spelling, "Vietnam," is used in reference to the war. I use the Vietnamese words, "Việt Nam," when referring to the country. To most Americans, particularly those who were alive during the 60s and 70s, Vietnam means a war. That unfortunate idea perpetuates the stereotype of the country as a horrible place. No other conflict in America's history uses the proper name of a country for the name of a war. It is the "Korean War," not the "Korea War." It is the "Spanish-American War," not the "Spain War." Because the proper name of the country is used rather than an adjective, it is not unusual to read newspaper articles about a "Vietnam era helicopter" or a "Vietnam veteran," but you will never read newspaper articles about a "Korea era tank" or "Germany veteran." War and the word "Vietnam" are deeply intertwined. I have used the two different spellings to help readers differentiate between the country of today and the war of the past.

I make no apologies for my having been an infantry officer. I was proud of my service during the war, and am proud of it now. I volunteered for Vietnam, and served two tours of duty, the first tour as a lieutenant with the 199th Light Infantry Brigade in 1967, and the second in 1969–70, as a captain with the 1st Cavalry Division. Though I was awarded little bits of colored ribbon, the only award I am truly proud of is the Combat Infantryman's Badge. It means I was a grunt—the guy on the ground with a rifle—the man around whom all other parts of the military were created to support

During my second tour in 1969, I commanded Company C, 2nd Battalion, 5th Cavalry Regiment of the 1st Cavalry Division. My radio call sign was Tall Comanche 6, and Comanche6 is my email address today. If a reader thinks that this book is somehow an apology for my service, or that I am ashamed of my service, he or she is mistaken.

After leaving the army in 1970, I married fellow veteran Cindy Mason, who had served as an army nurse at the 24th Evacuation Hospital. Both of us also served in the National Guard during the early 1980s.

With the exception of an occasional brush with awkward memories—such as the American incursion into Cambodia in 1971 or the day in 1975 when Saigon fell—neither Cindy nor I thought much about the war. Years after the war, I had a friend at work who also had been a grunt. Jeff Wilhoit and I had philosophical conversations about our being neither happier nor less happy when we were humping 125 pounds of "stuff" on our backs than we were with mortgaged homes and car notes, but the reality was that for many years, I really didn't think about Vietnam very much, and neither did Cindy.

We were just boring, normal people.

It was the Internet that started things. As a career move, I saw a totally new medium arrive, and I saw the potential for using it to teach. New software came on the market that allowed me to create an actual course for free.

"Hey Cindy—I can create an online course, but I don't know what the course should be about. Any ideas?"

"Yeah—write a course about the Vietnam War—that's something you know a lot about."

I was to find out that I really didn't know much about it. My only knowledge was my own experience, and even there, my poor memory failed me. I had been a history major in college, so I began reading—lots of reading. I soon accumulated a rather large library of books about the war.

One night, while trying to find more information, I discovered the web site of the 1st Cavalry Division Association. There was a Guest Book on the site. I left a little comment about having served with Company C, 2nd Battalion, 5th Cavalry in 1969. Not a big deal.

Months passed. Frankly, I forgot about the comment, until an e-mail appeared one day from a guy who said he, too, had served with C 2/5 Cav in 1969.

Ah, fate. That's how I met Jim "Tree" Machin for the second time. Jim went on to organize reunions for the company—a rather unusual endeavor, since most reunions are big affairs for a whole division. I had never attended one of the big reunions, because I doubted I would find anybody I had served with.

The first company reunion was in Atlanta in 2000. It was a lot of fun, and Jim asked me to start a web site—and another obsession began, this time with creating the history and stories of Charlie Company during its six and a half years of combat in Vietnam. The web site can be found at www.tallcomanche.org.

As I rummaged around the Internet in search of more history, the web fed me again—this time in finding the site of an organization that organized trips back to Việt Nam.

"Hey Cindy—you wanna go back to Việt Nam?"

"Hell, no!"

But she mellowed.

She had tried to mend the broken bodies of young men back in 1969—sometimes without success. Many of her patients back then were paralyzed—10 percent died on her ward, despite the medical team's best efforts. I saw a fair amount of death in the infantry—she saw it on a daily basis. When actor Christopher Reeve (who played Superman in the movie) was thrown from his horse and paralyzed, Cindy was vividly reminded again of the loss she saw every day in Vietnam.

We knew the country must have changed, but we had no idea how it had changed. I somehow knew I wouldn't find Landing Zone (LZ) Ike again, but maybe something would be left of some of the other places we'd been. Cindy pretty much assumed there wouldn't be much left of Long Binh post, stripped of all the wiring, plumbing, sheet metal and concrete, but she read the newspaper story of an army physician who had returned and found what he thought had once been the water tower for the 24th Evacuation Hospital. We both were curious to know what Việt Nam would be like at peace. Like many veterans, we had thought the country beautiful even during the war.

She mellowed enough—and I sent an e-mail to Chuck Ward, asking for more information about the trips his organization conducted. Conjecture led to real discussion, then to plans. Cindy had lengthy phone conversations with Joette Ward, who assured her that the Vietnamese would not be shooting at her, and that she wouldn't be eating meals from a mess kit.

With excited anticipation and nervous suspicion, Cindy and I first returned to Việt Nam in 2002 for a two-week medical aid project organized by Vets With A Mission (www.vwam.com), an excellent organization that seeks to reconcile veterans with their experiences during the war. I made a second trip by myself in March, 2003, to work with the University of Đa Nẵng for three weeks, and then we both spent a marvelous two-week vacation in Việt Nam during the summer of 2003.

After I retired in December, 2004, we went back to Việt Nam a fourth time. This trip lasted for one and a half years. We lived in the city of Huế (say *hway*), where we taught English at the university.

We continue to travel back to see friends and work on other projects. We take great delight that some of our former students are now either doing graduate work at American universities, or have completed their studies in the United States.

The Return

The author sharing some moments with rice harvesters in the fields southeast of Huế that once produced food for the emperor.

Photo courtesy Phan Cu

Are you crazy? Are you out of your mind? You might step on a booby trap or something."

The professor stopped in his tracks when I told him I was going to retire, then go live and teach in Việt Nam. Like me, he was a veteran of the war there—he had been an artillery forward observer with the U.S. Marine Corps. Forty years later, he was looking forward to retirement. He had come home from the war, earned his Ph. D. in biology, and had been a researcher for the government as well as a professor at a university. He's a smart man.

And he could not imagine I would actually go live in Việt Nam.

I seem to get two reactions from Vietnam vets when they hear I have been there recently—and that I actually lived there for a year and a half. They either want to go back too—or they think I am out of my mind. I've noticed the ones who want to go back tell me so surreptitiously.

I'd wanted to go back for years. As I am blessed with a poor memory, I have few of the haunting dreams that plague other veterans. I wanted to see what the place was like, now that the country is at peace. Many vets want nothing to do with the place.

I have a theory as to why many vets don't want to go back.

Have you ever gone to a high school reunion? Or college reunion? Or a reunion of fellow veterans? If your reaction to your first

First Lieutenant Doug Young, 199th Light Infantry Brigade, outside the bucolic village of Binh Chanh in 1967. Today Bình Chánh is a suburban industrial park and part of Hồ Chí Minh City.

21

Though the name was changed to Hồ Chí Minh City in 1976, most people still call it Sài Gòn. The central part of the city, as seen during the short taxi ride from Tân Sơn Nhất airport.

reunion was, *Who in the hell invited all these old people?* then you know why vets are leery of returning to Vietnam. Your memories of school chums are rooted in the "old days," but while your memories stay the same, you have grown and moved on. Our memories of Vietnam stay rooted in the past too. We vets are comfortably middle-aged now (or older), yet the Vietnam in our minds is the Vietnam of our youth. It remains a land of large convoys of deuce-and-a-half trucks, of helicopters, of the reeking smell of decay in the cities, and the smell of burning human waste on the fire bases. Our minds remember flares in the night sky, and Coke girls outside the villages.

But just as people move on after high school, Việt Nam[1] has moved on too. Reminders of the war are hard to find. Those sandbags we laboriously filled for bunkers are long gone. Creaky old French buildings in Saigon have been replaced by concrete and glass skyscrapers. Most of the dirt-floored wattle huts in the villages have been replaced by small concrete and brick houses. Because 70 percent of the population has been born since the war ended in 1975, most people have no memory of the war. Vietnamese youth are like American youth—they think wars are for old men to tell stories about.

---

1 Just as I use two spellings for the country, so too do I refer to war-time Saigon and present day Sài Gòn.

Today a returning vet will see a bustling country. The people want "the good life" for their children just as we do. Yes—the government is still Communist, and that is a hobble, but any returning veteran will be struck by the incredible beauty of a place that is now at peace, and a people who are the same by night as they are by day.

And you won't even see an AK-47 rifle.

Left: A young employee at the Cu Chi tunnels shows tourists how a spider hole worked during the war. Center: Old American military hardware on display at an outdoor museum in Hué. Right: The museum at Khe Sanh—this is all there is except for old Huey and Chinook helicopters, a bunker made of nylon sandbags filled with concrete, and a howitzer with the tires rotted off.

If a veteran wants to go back to Vietnam to see his old fire base or other memories of the war, there is some good news and some bad news.

The good news is that anything to do with the war is either in a tourist site or in a museum.

The bad news is that anything to do with the war is either in a tourist site or in a museum.

Not quite everything is gone, but the "war things" are very hard to find, even if they are in plain view.

In plain view in unexpected places.

Homesickness took hold of Cindy and me during the first weeks we lived in Hué in 2005. We'd certainly eaten Vietnamese food before—in fact we both liked Vietnamese food—but we were in the first throes of missing home, and needed some American comfort food. We'd both learned to eat with chopsticks during the war, but we wanted to sit down at a table and use a knife, fork, and spoon. Maybe a place where somebody spoke English—and maybe a place with somebody our own age.

Julie, our American teaching teammate, had taken us to the Mandarin Café during the first few days in Hué, but we were so new to living in Việt Nam that we were a little disappointed—it wasn't "Vietnamese enough"—it was a backpacker café geared for Western tourists. But one night, when that first bout of homesickness hit us, not being "Vietnamese enough" was a good thing, and we decided to go the Mandarin again for dinner. They served Western food at the Mandarin (or at least what the cooks thought Western food should taste like)—spaghetti bolognaise, BLT sandwiches, baked potatoes with butter, and similar fare. The place had good write-ups in *The Lonely Planet,* and the owner, Mr. Cu (say *Coo*), lived up to his reputation as a chatty English speaker. After ordering our food, we talked with Cu awhile. When the food was served, we took knives and forks from the table top holder. The knife was the typical yellow handled cheapie knife, and as expected, the spoon was flimsy tin.

But the fork—the fork was solid. I noticed it was solid, but didn't think much more about it.

Months passed, and we kept going back to the Mandarin. Each time we ate there, I would scrounge around in the holder until I found one of those nice, solid forks. They felt so much like home. Chopsticks were what I used when eating Vietnamese food, but when eating Western food, I wanted to use Western utensils. One night, Cu saw me looking for a solid fork, and joined us at our table.

"You like my forks?" He had the kind of grin on his face that told me I was about to learn something.

"Yeah—they're like American forks—really solid."

And I was told American lips had passed over them before. Cu found them in a small village market—they were from an old U.S. Army mess hall. The storekeeper had long sold out of knives and spoons, but she had lots of forks left to sell. Why? Because the Vietnamese use spoons and knives, but not forks—they use chopsticks—and that's why many of the forks at the Mandarin Café are stamped "U.S. Army."

I doubt if many veterans have fond memories of something as mundane as mess hall forks, nor do I think they would have fond memories of some of the other war remnants I found. The longer I lived in Việt Nam, the more remnants I found.

Over a year after discovering the American forks, I found another set of war relics out in the open. I saw lots of them every day. They were all over the Perfume River and on its numerous tributaries. Little small boats—used by fishermen, water taxis, kids, and women going to market. They were as common as motorbikes. Again, it was Cu who told me—and as he did with the forks, he had a twinkle in his eye that said he enjoyed watching his American friend learn something that was obvious to him.

During the war, American jet fighters jettisoned their external fuel tanks when they were empty. Enterprising Vietnamese retrieved them from the jungle, cut them in half, and covered the sharp edges with wood. The aluminum boats are almost indestructible, and are ubiquitous in central Việt Nam. Cu had been one of those who made the boats after 1975 when the Communists took over—he did it to feed his family.

If a returning vet gets off the tourist streets, there are a few other reminders to be found. In one section of Huế, there are still some concrete bunkers. Of course, these were built by South Vietnamese troops, who used concrete because they assumed they would be there awhile. American forces built most fortifications with sand bags, because we knew we would be going home. Today, the bunkers are littered with trash, covered by vines and posters—and ignored by everybody.

Her boat was once the external fuel tank of an American fighter plane. The ducklings she is herding will be dinner in a few months. Ducks raised for food don't fly more than a few feet, so she is in little danger of losing them.

But there is no use trying to find Camp Evans or LZ Ike or Firebase Tomahawk. Phuoc Vinh is now a sleepy village again, and Long Binh is an industrial park. There is a bucolic village at the foot of The Rockpile, and Phú Bài is Huế's commercial airport. The airstrip at Cam Ranh Bay is now the busy terminal for tourists on the way to Nha Trang. China Beach is overrun with four- and five-star resorts and golf courses. While taxiing to the gate at today's Tân Sõn Nhất International Airport in Hồ Chí Minh City, your airplane will pass by a few old American revetments that once sheltered warplanes and helicopters—and that may give the returning veteran the false hope that his memories will be found too.

But a veteran's memories are just that—memories.

Call it "Returning Vet Syndrome." With so many less-than-happy memories of a place that had a huge impact on one's life, it takes a little while for a veteran to digest the differences between memory and the present.

Our first return trip in 2002 was with a group of other veterans. We flew from Los Angeles to Hong Kong, then into Sài Gòn from there. Tired and jet lagged, I found that my confidence began to erode as we flew closer to Việt Nam. Yes—my intellect knew the country would have changed in thirty-two years, but I

The Đông Ba (say Dome Bah) Gate into the Citadel section of Huế was pulverized during the Tet Offensive of 1968. It was crudely rebuilt by the old southern government, but with an ugly concrete bunker on top. Since this photo was taken in 2005, the top of the gate has been rebuilt sans bunker.

didn't know how it would have changed. As we approached the coast, with an hour or so to think before landing, my imagination went wild. Was it silly of me to think that the immigration officers might be looking for returning veterans? I crazily imagined being hauled off for questioning by some cruel NVA[2] colonel who sought revenge because I had been an American infantryman. Maybe they had a database of all the Americans who had ever served in Vietnam.

Maybe somebody remembers…

Who knows if someone sees me who…

See the 1st Cav emblem on my pen…

---

2 North Vietnamese Army, the American name for the People's Army of Vietnam. The NVA should not be confused with the Vietcong, a separate armed force composed primarily of southerners.

After we got off the 747 and entered the big immigration processing area, I looked around for a soldier with an AK-47, but there was none. While standing in line, waiting to be checked in through Immigration, I discovered that the pain in the palms of my hands was caused by my fingernails. I was actually a little disappointed when the young immigration official behind the counter merely compared me to my passport photo, typed something into his computer, noisily stamped my passport, and handed it back to me as he yelled, "Next!"

So much for worrying about being regarded as "The Enemy." I unclenched my fists, and started to look around to see the changes.

Though renamed Hồ Chí Minh City, most people still call the city Sài Gòn. In 1967, my unit had operated south of the city. When I came out of the field after nine months as a platoon leader, and became the company executive officer, I often drove between the firebase in the south and the main base north of Saigon. Back then, the city was choked with American Army trucks, Vietnamese peasant refugees, GI bars, hookers, blue Renault taxis, three-wheeled Lambretta minitrucks, gazillions of bicycles, and "The Smell."

But in 2002, on that very first trip back since the war, the drive into the downtown area was strange. I was seeing glass and concrete skyscrapers, streets filled with modern Japanese automobiles, and millions of motorbikes. People were dressed in casual Western clothes—not in some imagined "Asian style," and certainly not in black pajamas. Billboards touted Sony televisions, Toyota cars, Levi's jeans, shampoo, and other necessities of the good life.

Obviously, there were lots of changes in the country—but then again, some things were exactly the same, only different.

Following pages: The Continental Hotel was built by the French in 1880, and was the center of French social life in Saigon until Việt Nam won its independence in 1954. During the Vietnam War, most international correspondents stayed there.

Đồng Khởi Street (pronounced Dom Koy and translated as "Popular Uprising") was known as Tu Do Street (pronounced Too Doe, meaning Freedom) while the Americans were there. Few GIs were able to sample its many sins, but most had heard of the street, famous for its bars, prostitutes, and "Saigon Tea."

The Continental housed author Graham Greene when he wrote "The Quiet American," and you can see the hotel in the 1958 movie of the same name. Early scenes of "Indochine," starring Catherine Deneuve, also showed the place.

Today it is a four-star hotel right in the heart of the city.

Cindy was assigned to the Neurosur-gery Wards at the 24th Evacuation Hospital in Long Binh. Nothing of the hospital exists today, though Long Binh Post, once the largest American military post outside the United States, is now an industrial park.

A favorite tourist destination in Hồ Chí Minh City is Reunification Palace—known as Independence Palace when it was the home of the presidents of the old South Vietnam. Bright young ladies dressed in ào dài (say ow yie) take Westerners on guided tours through the building, which has been pre-served as it was when the south fell on April 30, 1975.

And it was in the basement that Cindy found a medicine cabinet like the ones she used during the war.

Memories, yes—but in a museum.

Đồng Khởi Street is lined with expensive stores patronized by Vietnamese and foreigners alike. Tourists flock to the central area, where the French colonial Sài Gòn Opera House (which once housed the lower house of the South Vietnamese legislature) vies with the towers of the Cara-velle Hotel. Drivers wait patiently next to the luxury auto-mobiles owned by their employers.

The Bitexo Financial Tower, as seen while under construction in 2010, rises sixty-eight floors above the downtown area of Hồ Chí Minh City, making it the tallest structure in the city, dwarfing the other tall buildings that have replaced most of the low slung buildings of the French era

During the first trip in 2002, we stayed at the Rex Hotel in Hồ Chí Minh City, but I'd been to the Rex before. During the war, it was a BOQ[3] for senior officers—think of it as a residential long-term hotel for colonels and generals. It was also where the infamous Five O'clock Follies took place—the press conferences that always told upbeat stories for public consumption. The Rex Hotel had a bar on the roof—a nice bar. You could order a beer, then look down at the street and watch the traffic circling the intersection, or you could look at the sky and watch the flares and tracers from distant firefights. Whether you watched the traffic or the firefights, you were isolated from the action.

The colonels loved the rooftop bar at the Rex. Dressed in starched khakis, they had a good life. They commuted to their offices to work. That's why we grunts called them "Strap Hangers," like their subway-riding commuter cousins back in America. As a lieutenant in 1967, I was technically allowed in the Officer's Club, but was hardly welcome. I was rather proud that my boots had never seen polish; I was a grunt—a fighter—most certainly not a spit-and-polish office worker.

On one of my trips through the city, between our firebase and the main base, I got thirsty. I wanted a beer. And I wanted to drink that beer in the rooftop bar at the Rex.

I parked the muddy jeep nearby, slung my M-16 rifle over my shoulder, and returned the salute of the Military Police standing guard in the sandbagged bunker at the entrance. Unpolished boots, semi-clean uniform, steel helmet, loaded M-16 and all, I got on the elevator to the roof.

There were a lot of stares from the Strap Hangers as I walked over to the bar and ordered a beer. But after all, what could they do? Send me to The Nam?

One of the best beers I ever had.

Fast forward to 2002—thirty-five years later, I drank another beer at the Rex Hotel rooftop bar.

Maybe the second best beer I ever had.

But if the rooftop bar at the Rex was the same, only different—some things were completely gone.

Ask a veteran—ask if he remembers "The Smell." Watch the smile of remembrance on his face.

Back in 1966, on my very first tour of duty in Vietnam, I had noticed a smell even before the plane landed. No—not the smell of human waste being burned with diesel fuel, but rather the smell of the cities and villages.

In 2002, as our airplane circled Sài Gòn in preparation for landing, I wondered when I would smell "The Smell."

---

3 Bachelor Officer's Quarters. Duty in Vietnam was an "unaccompanied tour," which meant that spouses did not live with the service members. Because all married men were "geographic bachelors," senior officers who were not assigned to field units slept in a BOQ.

When I didn't smell anything while walking on the jet way from the plane to the terminal, I figured it was because unpleasant jet fumes masked it.

When I didn't smell anything in the Immigrations and Customs area, I figured it was because of the air conditioning.

I didn't smell it in the baggage area either. I figured I would smell it once I got outside, but during the short walk from the air-conditioned terminal to the air-conditioned bus, I didn't smell it.

It wasn't until I was standing on a busy street corner in Sài Gòn, waiting for Cindy to finish shopping, that I figured why "The Smell" was gone. I watched a city worker sweeping leaves from the gutter, and I realized that the Sài Gòn of today is clean. As my wife observed, there were no refugees living in the street now—no garbage in the gutters, and no human waste in the numerous canals and rivers. Việt Nam is at peace, and there is no "Smell" anymore.

Nguyễn Huệ (say *nwin hway*) Street is a very busy boulevard in Hồ Chí Minh City, with typical big city crowds. I tried to stroll down its sidewalks, but found I was just pushed along by the mass of humanity, so I stepped aside and people-watched for awhile. Lively and talkative, the young urban professionals walking by contrasted strongly with the people I had seen only a few miles away in 1967, in a village named Binh Chanh.

Binh Chanh in the war years was a small farming village surrounded by rice paddies and hamlets. It was on Route Four, the major highway heading south from Saigon into the Mekong River delta. My unit was part of the 199th Light Infantry Brigade, which served as palace guard for the capital city.

Our company set up in a blasted-out schoolhouse on one of the farm roads leading into the village, and our little encampment straddled the road. Our job was the original "Mission Impossible"—we were somehow supposed to winnow out the bad guys from the peasants who just wanted to be left alone.

I didn't want to play poker with these peasants—their faces never betrayed any emotion. We often provided security for the South Vietnamese Military Police as they swept villages, checking ID cards. I was amazed at the people's stoicism—they took a lot of harassment from the MPs (or White Mice, as we called them). In the evenings, as we went out on patrol, some would peek out the doorways of their hovels. They watched the big men with the guns go by, and then waited for the night, when the Vietcong would visit. The peasants' life was a hard one.

Back then, the streets were filled with mama-sans going to work. (American soldiers called adult women "mama-san"—the term was a carryover from GIs who had served in Korea.) Many of the women worked at American bases, doing laundry or cleaning quarters. Cindy's nurses' quarters had such women. They were also called "hooch maids," a hooch being the slang term for any place Americans lived. Most of the hooch maids had been uprooted from their homes by the war, and now lived in squatter camps in the cities or outside American base camps. They swept floors, washed uniforms, and shined boots. They interacted as little as possible with the Americans, except to fend off the occasional amorous advance—and they showed little reaction when doing that, except for giggly embarrassment.

The crowd passing by on Nguyễn Huệ Street showed none of the stoicism I had seen in the peasants or mama-sans in 1967. Today there was nothing to be stoic about. Nor were they impoverished. If they saw me at all, they ignored me—a Western foreigner is neither unusual nor a threat to anyone in today's cities. Yes, there are street vendors on Nguyễn Huệ Street, but they aren't necessarily poor. They aren't living on the largesse of American soldiers either—they are either selling tourist stuff to the many Westerners who come to Việt Nam, or are selling food to the tourism workers.

What was once the small village of Binh Chanh is now an industrial park, filled with soup factories and supermarkets. The old two-lane Route Four is now a six-lane divided highway with electrical lines running down the center.

Thinking of Binh Chanh then, and seeing the Bình Chánh of today—thinking of the people I saw in 1967 and seeing the people of today—I began to truly realize the war was over.

It was not the last time I was to have that thought.

After seeing the changes to Sài Gòn, I found that the smaller cities have changed too. Huế is a city of about 350,000, and was the epicenter of the 1968 Tet Offensive. Today's Huế has a new shopping plaza that sports a Kentucky Fried Chicken outlet. The beautiful old Trương Tiền (say *True-ong Tee-in*) Bridge had its two northern spans dropped into the river by Communist forces in 1968. Today, the bridge has been rebuilt and the southern end is a gathering spot for young lovers.

But most veterans never saw the cities, much less Saigon—they were out "humping the weeds" in the rice fields and jungles, and they were moving warily through the villages. They were out in the countryside. Today, there aren't any Gucci stores in the countryside, but change is still very evident.

The cities of Việt Nam are booming—coming apart at the seams—but 70 percent of the population still lives in rural areas. This is a different Việt Nam than seen in the cities. The nation is long past the time when people lived in deep poverty and were starving. Today, most countryside folk live in concrete houses, have a motorbike and television set, and send their kids to school. Nonetheless, the farmer's life of today is a hard one, but without the dangers and hassles of a war going on in the fields.

Even when venturing deep into the mountains and looking hard for a wattle hut—the grass and stick shack soldiers saw during the war—the veteran will find electricity (and televisions) in all of them, and his mobile phone will have five pegs.

Cindy and I differ from many American couples. Most veterans of the Vietnam War are men, but Cindy is a veteran too—she was a nurse at the 24th Evacuation Hospital in Long Binh. There aren't many Vietnam veterans married to other Vietnam veterans.

In 1969, during my second tour, I did not come near the huge Long Binh post until I was reassigned out of the field and took a new job as the S1 (administration officer) of our battalion. Part of my job was to be sure we got the right personnel to replace losses caused by those who were wounded, had been killed in action, or had finished their tour. Every two weeks or so, I would climb into my jeep with a driver, and we'd head to the 1st Cavalry Division's rear area at Bien Hoa (say *Behn Wah*). I'd ride "shotgun," while John or Kenny

Notice the screening around the business in the top photo— it was to keep out grenades. The trash in the street helped cause The Smell. The thatched roof hut in the bottom photo was very common during the war years.

dodged the convoys and ox carts. I usually finished my work too late in the day for us to drive back to our base camp—one simply did not drive the roads of wartime Vietnam at night. We would get bunks at the 90th Replacement Battalion, find some food, and drive back the next day.

Specialist Ken Gardiner and I were sharing a beer (hard to do in the rear areas, where officers and enlisted men were not supposed to socialize), when an idea came to me. I suggested to Kenny that we go see some round-eyed women.

Reaching across the table, Kenny pulled my can of beer away, telling me, "I think you've had enough, Captain."

"No no, Kenny. There's a hospital nearby. I was there during my first tour, when I had malaria. Really—there are American nurses there."

In a few minutes, we were at the 24th Evacuation Hospital. Using my made-up story of trying to find a wounded "Sergeant Smith" from my unit, I went into each ward, only to be met by a male each time.

No fun meeting guys! I wanted to meet a round-eyed woman!

I wandered into X-Ray, the lab tech's office, and two or three other buildings. I saw a few women in the background, but it was always a male who approached me to ask if I needed help.

Below: Originally built by the French in the late 1890s, the Trương Tiền bridge was designed by Gustave Eiffel of Eiffel Tower fame, and was named Pont Clémenceau for Georges Clémenceau, then Prime Minister of France. Reviled at the time as a symbol of colonialism, today it is one of the landmarks of the city. The bridge is in use today—mainly by motorbikes and bicycles, because the weight of automobiles puts too much stress on the old structure.

Note the electricity wires into the house, the tile roofs and the concrete walkways. Though not comfortable by American standards, peasant housing is infinitely better than it was during the war.

I finally told Kenny that I would try one more building. I spotted a door that was decorated with the unit patches of the various units the hospital served, and I walked into Ward Five.

And I got sober fast.

Each bed had a name card above it, detailing the wounded man's name and rank, along with the unit patch. And there were a lot of 1st Cav patches above those beds, most occupied by men with very serious wounds. Many were swaddled with gauze and tape, with elevated limbs in casts. Most had heavy bandages wrapped around their heads, with only closed eyes showing. Tubes ran in and out of all of them. Somebody in The Cav had been in a hell of a big fight.

As I stood in the middle of the ward, obviously taken aback by the carnage in the room, a pert blond approached.

"Good evening, Sir."

"What is this place, Lieutenant?"

Sensing my anxiety, Second Lieutenant Cynthia Mason went for the throat.

"Sir—welcome to the world's only vegetable garden that waters itself."

The juxtaposition of old and new is everywhere—farmers plowing rice paddies near Củ Chi,(say Coo Chee) and cell phones in the mountains. Even the dress of the farmer on the tractor belies the common image of Việt Nam—his baseball cap and work boots are similar to what an American farm worker would wear

I had stumbled on to the Neurosurgery Ward, one of two such places in the entire combat zone of South Vietnam. If a wounded soldier had been hit in the face or the spinal cord, he went to Wards Five and Six of the 24th Evac. It's where the paralyzed and the head trauma patients were taken.

Cindy wasn't being crude or out-of-bounds, though she impishly enjoyed seeing a cocky infantry captain squirm a little. The rest of the hospital staff called Wards Five and Six "The Vegetable Garden." Those working on the wards used the same moniker simply as dark humor—a way to relieve the stress of working twelve-hour shifts caring for patients with a very high mortality rate. It's where twenty-one-year-old nurses cared for nineteen-year-old soldiers.

I was smitten immediately. Though obviously the military phone lines were meant for military work, and as long as we ignored the fact that five or six switchboard operators were listening to our conversations, we quickly built on the attraction of that first night. It took a special brand of nurse to work on The Vegetable Garden, and Cindy was special enough to marry in 1971.

Cindy was the first truly wonderful thing to come out of my two tours of duty in Vietnam.

Christmas Day, 1969, at the 24th Evacuation Hospital. The staff treated a large group of Vietnamese orphans to a party, complete with Christmas presents and a big meal. Cindy normally worked six days a week on twelve-hour shifts, but she swapped out with someone on that day to spend time with me. I couldn't wear civilian clothes as she could, but I did put on clean fatigues. Little did we know in 1969 that we would still be holding hands in Việt Nam thirty-six years later.

Photo courtesy Barbara Crookshank

Our marriage has always included a bond springing from our experiences in Vietnam. Seeing the huge changes to the country during that first return trip in 2002 trip whetted our appetite to know more about Việt Nam. We saw the country with new eyes, and we liked it.

While still on that two-week humanitarian medical trip to Đa Nẵng, I took a busman's holiday from working in the clinic to visit the University of Đa Nẵng. I wanted to visit my counterpart at a Vietnamese university—and see how a school on the other side of the world worked. Besides being treated like royalty, I was given a nice lunch and paid a visit by the Director of International Affairs. He wanted to know if I would retire and come to the University of Đa Nẵng to teach. Though flattered, I declined.

But I was able to arrange for an official trip the following year, as a representative of my employer. Because the trip would be paid for with taxpayer funds, I could not take Cindy with me. I arrived in March, 2003, and spent three weeks working with Mr. Dung (say *yoom*) in Đa Nẵng. Part of our work took us to smaller cities such as Qui Nhơn, Quảng Ngãi and Phan Rang, all of which played prominent roles in the war. Though occupied with work, social meetings and tours of campuses, I kept an eye peeled for

SAME RIVER, DIFFERENT WATER

anything having to do with the war. The only time I saw anything was while visiting the ancient Cham[4] towers outside Phan Rang. In the distance I saw military aircraft taking off and landing at what once had been an American air base.

Later, in the summer of 2003, Cindy and I took a two-week vacation in Việt Nam. Though we have since taken many trips to Việt Nam, this was the only trip we took during which we actually tried to find places we had been during the war. During the first trip in 2002, we just tried to digest the differences we'd seen since the thirty-five years of our absence. During the second trip in 2003, we got that out of our system—we looked for reminders of the war, but finding few of them, our eyes were opened to the beauty of a wonderful country.

We were changing—we were becoming people who loved being in Việt Nam for its own sake, not merely to try to find memories of war.

As the wheels came up on our plane and Tân Sõn Nhất airport fell away, we held hands as we looked out the window. When the lights were gone, we looked at each other and agreed our destiny lay in Việt Nam. We didn't know when, and we didn't know how.

We just knew we would be back for more than a vacation.

What we didn't know was that we were continuing a journey together that began in 1969.

(Following pages) The Vietnamese normally remove their footwear before entering a home. These pre-schoolers follow the same custom while in school. However, at the university where we taught, everyone wore their shoes in the classroom.

While living in Việt Nam, removing my shoes was one custom I disliked, but I dutifully took my shoes off when visiting someone. In our apartment, I removed my shoes or sandals, but wore rubber flip-flops just to ease my feet on the hard tile floors.

Strangely, removing my street shoes when entering my home is the one Vietnamese custom I observe now that I am back in America.

---

4 The Cham people were once the predominant rulers of today's central Việt Nam. They were an advanced civilization with strong Hindu and Indian influences. Eventually the Vietnamese conquered the Cham kingdom, and all that remains are some towers, a museum in Đa Nẵng, and a small ethnic minority

One and a half years after our vacation, Cindy and I arrived in the city of Huế to make it our home. It was cold and rainy that day in February, 2005—typical for that time of year—but we didn't know it was typical. We'd been in the southern area of the country, back in the 1960s. The rainy season around Saigon meant afternoon thunderstorms, with temperatures varying from hot to hotter. We were truly unprepared for the damp chill and constant mist of the Huế winter.

We were picked up at the airport and brought into the city by two teachers of the university we had contracted with. As the Toyota van whizzed down the highway, I pondered my new home. *"What in the hell have you done to yourself, Doug?"* I said inwardly, as I saw unexplained little toy-like houses outside people's homes. The van passed motorbikes with two or three people on board—everybody clad in ponchos to ward off the rain. Unable to speak or read Vietnamese, I couldn't understand the signs on businesses. Many of the houses had their doors open, and I could look inside to see people eating at low tables. The scene passing by the van was very different from America.

I had heard Vietnamese people say that Huế is a beautiful city—the jewel of the country, known for its royal buildings and the Perfume River. What I saw in the first few days was anything but beautiful—I saw moldy walls, uneven sidewalks, peeling paint, crumbling plaster, and rusty metal. Huế seemed ugly—not pretty.

But despite the rain and the grubby appearance, our first few weeks were great. Our students were all eager to learn from their new American teachers. Every meal was something new. Faculty welcomed us—our American teammates, Julie and Hang (a Vietnamese-American), were great. Every day was an adventure.

But we had indeed made a mistake—we believed that just because we had traveled in Việt Nam on vacation, we would know something about how to live in the place. We didn't expect any problems living in the country.

It soon became obvious that we were going to have problems—lots of problems. We weren't tourists in Việt Nam anymore—we were living and working in Việt Nam. A different culture—a different way of seeing the world. You can read books, talk to people, and learn all about culture shock, but it is to no avail when you're actually in the new country—you just gotta go through it. You may even know, as we did, that the culture shock is coming, but that doesn't render the shock any less intense. The first few weeks were great—everything was new and exciting. It was like a honeymoon. But after a few weeks, we began to notice that the food wasn't exactly like Mom's home cooking—the traffic seemed crazy—people didn't seem to be punctual—people in Việt Nam didn't seem to care if our housing was adequate—and we got tired of pointing and smiling and speaking pidgin Vietnamese whenever we needed to communicate. The stress started to show a bit: "Dammit—why do the Vietnamese do *(fill in the blank)* this way?" After a while longer, we hit the culture shock wall.

This is Home?

That first semester at the University of Huế was tough on Cindy. We were housed on the top floor of a class-room building on the campus of the College of Pedagogy—what would be a Teacher's College in America. We had one room, eleven by nineteen feet—a very small area. It was furnished with a double bed (no mat-tress—just two thin foam pads), two upright wooden chairs suitable for interrogations or executions, and two bare fluorescent lightbulbs in the ceiling. The shower was moldy, but provided the only hot water in the flat. We shared a common room with the two other American teachers, as well as a two-burner "stove" and a washing machine.

It was harder on Cindy than on me because it changed her roles in life. She was used to running her house. Like many middle-aged married women, a large part of her identity was in running her home. Part of "home" is food. Cindy is an excellent cook—it's her hobby, and making a delicious meal is a skill she revels in. Inviting friends to share the meal is part of having a home. She couldn't do that in Việt Nam, because she had no real kitchen—no pots and pans—no oven—no way to store ingredients. Worse, she couldn't go shopping to buy the items she needed for cooking. Unable to speak Vietnamese, she couldn't ask someone where nutmeg could be found, or find the person who sold bacon or who sold flour.

Frustrated at not being able to cook, Cindy also had the embarrassment of not having a decent place for vis-iting students to sit—they had to sit on the bed, while we sat in one of the two chairs. Part of our work was to provide a place for our students to gather for after-hours activities and visits, but Cindy could not fulfill the role of hostess. We were still newbies in Việt Nam, so we didn't know that our digs were often better than our students' homes—we just saw things through our American eyes, and thought we were unable to be good hosts.

Though we had the washer, we didn't have a dryer. Hence, when we were doing the laundry, the room looked like a New York tenement, with clothes hanging everywhere a space could be found. With the misty rain and 99.5 percent humidity, the laundry took a long time to dry.

We didn't need the wheezy air conditioner at first, because the temperature hovered around fifty or sixty degrees, but as winter waned, we discovered Huế has only two seasons: it is either cold and wet, or it is hotter than the hubs of hell. My body's need to sweat required air conditioning, but the air conditioner often didn't work well, or didn't work at all. Another "luxury" was the mosquito netting on the bed. There is no problem with malaria in Huế, but there are mosquitoes. To avoid being awakened in the middle of the night by a buzzing in the ears, we used the netting.

Our housing package also included a fitness program—we lived on the fourth floor, and there was no eleva-tor. Our transportation was bicycles. The combination of pedaling, walking up four flights of stairs five to six times a day, the heat, and the strange new food caused us to lose a lot of weight. By the end of the first semester, I was fitter than I had been in years, but getting fit was hard and hungry work.

Watching Cindy struggle with her issues, and knowing I was impotent to help her, only made matters worse.

The Internet to the rescue.

Our teaching agency had a very smart lady who ran operations in Việt Nam. Sandy Harrison realized Cindy was a little older than the usual young and single expatriate American teacher—Cindy was a married woman who was used to enjoying her domestic duties. Sandy asked another middle-aged lady who had previously served in Việt Nam to mentor Cindy. Besides flying all the way to Thailand to help in our training, Nancy Farnum stayed in touch with Cindy after we arrived in Huế. She'd been through the same experience herself in Hà Nội—and she knew it was tough. Via e-mail, she instructed:

"Cindy—put your hands on the keyboard right now and we'll both pray about this."

"Cindy—don't worry about the people back home thinking less of you if you decide to come home."

"Cindy—this is so hard on you—and you need to give yourself permission to go home if you need to."

And that did it—Cindy gave herself permission to go home—and realized she did not want to go home. But it was just one battle—just one small part of overcoming culture shock.

Bicycle riding in heavy traffic on Lê Lọi Street trimmed a lot of weight.

Our room was on the top floor at the end of the building. There were class-rooms on the bottom floor and dormi-tories on the other side of the court-yard.

A young lady riding her bicycle on the wrong side of the street is normal traffic. She entered the main street from a side street. Rather than pulling into the intersection and waiting for traffic to clear before making her left turn, she merely rode down the street on the wrong side until a spot cleared and she could move over to the right.

Photo by Cindy Young

Chaos Theory – Otherwise Known as Vietnamese Traffic

Bicycles were the only way to get around in Huế during that spring of 2005. It had been some time since either of us had graced a bicycle seat, but we found the old adage about never forgetting how to ride to be true. After a couple of wobbly trips around the dorm courtyard, we were just fine. Well—maybe a little shaky in heavy traffic, but fine nonetheless.

Traffic in Việt Nam has been described using many different adjectives—chaotic is one of the kinder descriptions. Depending on the time of day, about 60 percent of the traffic is motorbikes and scooters. Motorbikes are not full-blown motorcycles—they have small engines and low gearing. They are designed to carry a lot of weight at a slow speed. Another 35 percent of the traffic is bicycles and *xích lôs*. (say *sick low*), three-wheeled pedaled vehicles intended to carry passengers or small freight. There were a few cars, vans, trucks, and buses.

Two old, overweight Americans, accustomed to driving air-conditioned cars with automatic transmissions, were now thrown into the craziness of Việt Nam's streets.

During the first week of teaching, I finished my class and pointed my bicycle back toward our room. In America, I'd been taught to hug the right curb when going slower than other traffic, but that didn't seem to work in Huế.

I saw the young lady on her bicycle coming toward me on a side street.

Damn! She had just turned onto my street—but she was on my side of the road, headed directly toward me! Now what was I supposed to do?

The girl solved the problem for me. Seeing that the traffic coming toward her had a hole in it, she merely crossed the street and pedaled along on the correct side of the street.

Muttering to myself that this was going to take some getting used to, I almost didn't see the kid on his motorbike racing toward me. Luckily, I had enough sense to just keep pedaling forward—and like the bicyclist, he found a way to get across the center line to the right side of the road.

It took me awhile to realize traffic in Huế moves at a slower pace than in America. It just seemed fast because I was used to being inside a quiet car, but in Huế, I was out in the open with the exhaust fumes, loud horns, and trucks. Except for the occasional kid blasting by at teenager speeds, most of the motorbikes move only a little bit faster than the bicycles. There is too much traffic for the big vehicles to go fast.

Việt Nam's traffic is first seen by a visitor from inside a bus or taxi, and though it seems insanity rules the road, there is a certain ebb and flow to the traffic—somewhat similar to watching a flock of birds fly. At some mystic cue, the birds will all change direction at the same time. So it is with traffic in Huế. While it seems chaotic at first, it actually has a flow to it. But the cue is not mystic. The secret of success is the horn.

That's right—the horn.

The only time I used my automobile horn in America was when I was angry at somebody who cut me off, or when I wanted the idiot who was stopped at the green traffic light to move, or when I wanted the farmer driving ten miles an hour under the speed limit to get out of my way. But in Việt Nam, the streets are a constant loud din of honking horns. Everybody seems obliged to honk three times every ten seconds.

The horn is used for an entirely different purpose in Việt Nam than in the United States. Think of it as driving by ear. As you are tooling along the street on your bike, you will hear the nice man on the motorbike approaching fast from your right rear, horn blaring. Good—you know he's there, and you don't swerve in front of him. Hear that deep-throated horn over your left shoulder? Probably a bus—or a truck. Yeah—better let him have the right of way. Didn't notice the motorbike coming out from a side street because your view was blocked? No problem—you can hear his horn. I never saw anyone give a middle finger salute in Việt Nam—horn honking is just the way things work.

My physical condition and my ability to handle the traffic both improved as the first weeks went by. Sometime in April, I narrowly missed being hit by a motorbike—and I cussed the kid because he *didn't* honk!

I Really Want to Eat (*Fill in the Blank*) Tonight—But I Don't Want to Get Wet

We had arrived in the middle of the rainy season. The constant rain and dampness only made the transition to living in Việt Nam that much harder. Because we had no kitchen and therefore no way for Cindy to cook, we ate lunch and dinner at restaurants. (Breakfast was peanut butter on toast, washed down with hot Lipton tea—we could fix that in our room.) We often walked over to the Mandarin Café in the rain—that's where we found the American forks—but we wanted to find other homey things.

Things like pizza.

Pizza was available from Little Italy. There were no Italian immigrants in Huế in 2005, but there was a Vietnamese who thought he knew what pizza should taste like. Our favorite was the "Four Cheese Pizza," or as we dubbed it, the Puddle of Cheese pizza. This stuff would hardly threaten Papa Giuseppe—or even Pizza Hut—but it tasted kinda like pizza, and that made it a comfort food.

Even better, Little Italy delivered! The rainy season in Huế can be miserable. When it isn't pouring rain, there is almost always a foggy mist in the air. While we rode our bicycles (and later, my motorbike) in the rain, sometimes it just wasn't fun. I'd peek my head out the apartment door, see that it wasn't raining, and then get on the motorbike, only to have a fine mist appear on my glasses. Those were the nights when the girls at Little Italy knew who Cindy was when she called in an order.

Vietnamese Girl at Little Italy on phone: "Hallo?"

Cindy: "I'd like to order a pizza."

Girl: "Ah! Mrs. Cindy! How are you tonight?" (Girlish giggle)

Cindy: "We would like a large Quattro Formaggio pizza, please? I want a 'Koe-kah' (Vietnamese way of saying "Coca-Cola") in a can."

Girl: "And Mr. Doug want Fanta in can?"

Cindy: "Yes."

And soon, a smiling young man, drenched to the bone, would appear at our door with a soggy cardboard box of pizza (now mostly cold), two cans of soft drinks—and a big smile. The kids would fight over who would bring our order. Tipping is unknown among the Vietnamese, so delivering to the Westerners who gave them as much money for one trip as they would make the rest of the entire night was great for them. On those cold rainy nights, they were more than happy to get on the motorbike, even if the two old Westerners weren't.

The Vietnamese don't cope with the rain—they grew up with it and treat it as a normal part of life. The rainy season in Huế lasts from mid-November to late February. Day after day, the sun does not shine, there is almost always a mist in the air, and downpours are frequent. The monsoon rains occur at different times of the year in different parts of the country.

On nights like this, after having been in the rain all day going to and from class, we missed having a dry and warm automobile—and we would telephone an order for pizza delivery.

It took a while, but eventually we grew to love Vietnamese food. As my Vietnamese friends can attest, my favorite food—Western or Vietnamese—is *phở* (say *fuh*), the marvelous beef noodle soup created for the gods. Cindy loves *bún thịt nướng* (say *boon tit nyew-ong*) to this day, but until our love affair with Vietnamese food began to happen, we looked all around Huế for Western food.

But the American forks and the pizza only delayed the inevitable—and culture shock was inevitable. We knew culture shock would come—but knowing it didn't make it easier. As one instructor told me during our training, "Asia has been here for five thousand years, and it ain't gonna change just because Doug Young showed up."

Time – Whatever That Is

It began to dawn on us just how different it was when we asked a faculty member about the end of the semester. We expected to hear a specific date. The answer we got was very different: "Oh, it depends. Depends on what year the student is in."

Okay—I could deal with that. The first-year (freshman) students began the semester first, followed a week later by the second-year students—and so on. A staggered beginning and end of a semester was understandable. No problem.

But the school would not give us dates for the beginning and end of a semester. Then we discovered the unpredictability of school holidays.

Unpredicted holidays? How could they not know beforehand about an upcoming holiday? But that is exactly what happened in late March, 2005. Pioneer Youth Day was on the calendar, but the government added a holiday to celebrate the thirtieth anniversary of the "liberation" of Huế. Worse, the students knew about it, but we got nothing official from the university. Just the class monitor[5] who told me the day prior to the holiday. Likewise, I was to find there was no definite date for the new school year to begin in late August. Returning students just showed up around the expected time, moved into their dorm rooms, then went to find out details. Nobody but us Americans were upset.

Long-term planning is not a strong suit of the Vietnamese. After living my American life as dictated by my Day Planner and having my day broken down into fifteen-minute segments, this was a tough difference to get used to.

Slowly we let Việt Nam change us. Việt Nam was teaching me lessons in life—good lessons. One of the first lessons I grasped was that I didn't need to micromanage my time.

In America, if I want to have lunch with a friend, I have to set it up at least two weeks in advance—e-mails sent—calendars checked—phone calls to the wife to be sure nothing else was going on—planning where we would eat lunch—suggesting a time, only to have the lunch partner say she can't make it then and suggest a time when I can't go…

You know the routine.

In Việt Nam, I might get home after teaching, think about meeting somebody for coffee, call that person on my cell phone—and meet him in thirty minutes at the Vỹ Dạ Xưa (say *vee ya soo-ah*) coffee house.

What happens if they can't come? Nothing. No great angst. We'll meet another time.

The head of the English department called a meeting—Tuesday at two o'clock. As dutiful punctual Americans, Cindy and I showed up at one forty-five. Since faculty members do not have offices (there is only one

---

5 The class monitor is a student, usually one of the very best students, who acts as a go-between for the class and the college on administrative issues. The title seemed scary to me at first—I wondered if the "class monitor" was some sort of government stooge whose sole function was to spy on me. Such were the fears I brought with me from my background.

large common office with a secretary and message board), we expected others would gather and help to arrange chairs in a classroom.

That didn't happen—we were the only ones there. At two o'clock (or so), somebody said the meeting would be in Room 210. With a lot of scraping sounds, a few men moved chairs, and the department chair arrived. There was no agenda—no planned topics—no designated people to speak on designated subjects—only a social time for thirty minutes or so. Finally, we began to talk about matters that affected us as teachers.

And that drove me nuts!

I seethed inside. To myself: "Not only can't they organize meetings the right way—they can't start them on time either. Supposing I had a three o'clock meeting—I would have been late for that because these chuckle-heads can't organize a meeting and be on time."

There is an academic way of describing the Vietnamese attitude—theirs is an event-based culture, not a time-based culture.

It means they put a premium on relationships—the social time beforehand was more important than the subjects to be covered in the actual meeting. Americans couldn't care less about "relationships" at a meeting—we have work to be done, so let's get going. To the Vietnamese, events only have a beginning time—not an ending time. Why? So they can finish the business the meeting had been called to conduct. To the Vietnamese, there is no sense in ending a meeting just because the clock says a certain time—they keep going until they have accomplished what the meeting was for in the first place. Are they worried that a long meeting might make you late for another appointment? No problem—the next group will wait until you can get there, or begin without you—not a big deal.

As the first two months began to slip by, the Vietnamese way of doing things was morphing from just annoying me to making me downright angry. On the bike ride back to my apartment that I knew was full of drying laundry, and knowing I would have to go out in the rain to find a place to eat, I was not a happy man.

Doing It the "American Way"

It was about six weeks into our time there when culture shock really hit us. As I mentioned earlier, Cindy had a tougher time than I did, but it was very hard for me to watch my wife cry—with the knowledge that there wasn't anything I could do to help her. I couldn't get her a nice house where she could entertain. She was washing dishes in the shower, because it had the only access to hot water. I couldn't help her learn to cook foods she had never seen before. She couldn't be "Grandma Cindy" to the kids at church—and there wasn't anything I could do about it.

And I wasn't having any luck teaching the Vietnamese to drive their motorbikes by the "normal" rules either. We finally found a place with "hamburgers," but they were dry and mealy—and the ketchup may have had the correct words on the bottle, but the stuff made in Singapore was nothing like the real ketchup back home. The patties weren't even served on a bun—they were on a baguette—a kind of French bread. That's not a hamburger—it's just a mystery meat sandwich!

We were conflicted—we loved our students (I am not being polite—we really loved our students). We loved teaching them. We were getting used to the food and the traffic—but hadn't adjusted to the Vietnamese way of doing things.

It wasn't that we regretted making the decision to live and teach in Việt Nam—but we missed the "normal" way of doing things. Being in our sixties amplified the problem. We were not quite as mentally flexible as our younger teammates—we were a little set in our ways.

Yeah—normal.

You know—the way we do things in America.

If you have a problem in America, you are expected to meet it head-on. If that problem is a person, meet that person and tell him directly what the problem is and how to fix it.

You know—look 'em in the eye.

After hearing for the third time that "someone" would come to fix our lethargic air conditioner, I decided to handle things the American way. "I'll show him! I'll show him how it's done. I'll show him the American way of getting things done. By damn, I was a manager for years in America—I know how to get things done!"

After calling the Rector (the Dean) of the College of Foreign Language on his cell phone—and catching him in a meeting—I knew I'd get some action. Yeah—he was upset, but that's how to get things done, eh?

You know—squeaky wheel gets the grease, and all that stuff.

At four in the afternoon, three men showed up at our room. None of them spoke English, and neither of our Vietnamese-speaking teammates were around. The three didn't seem to have the foggiest notion why they were there, but after some pointing and knob-turning, they seemed to understand that there was something the matter with the air conditioner. They hadn't brought any tools—not even a screw driver—so they changed the air filter and left.

Now I was really cranked! I didn't care if it was after working hours, I called the Rector again. He promised to send someone out "tomorrow," which of course meant trying to sleep in the muggy heat another night.

Tomorrow arrived, and so did three more men, one of whom seemed to be the boss, and who could speak a few words of English. This time, the crew brought a screw driver, a small hammer, and some Allen wrenches. After much fiddling around and many smiles aimed at me (which I did not return), they left. The air conditioner worked.

For a while.

A week after I made my first phone call, a competent repairman finally arrived. All that the unit needed was a fresh shot of coolant, but it had taken the persistent calls to the Rector to get it done. Each group that came by to "repair" the unit was composed of underlings who had neither the organizational authority nor the cultural impetus to make decisions. Before anything could be done, we had to peel off the layers.

This was the point where culture shock almost broke me. I was convinced of the superiority of the American culture and the stupidity of the Vietnamese. I ranted—I raved—I got depressed—I was frustrated.

I wanted to go home.

Cindy did too.

The food wasn't like home—and besides, Cindy couldn't cook like she did back home, because she couldn't shop in the market without knowing Vietnamese.

The ingredients weren't there anyway—and there was only a crummy little two-burner table top "stove."

The traffic be damned—the Vietnamese didn't follow any rules—stop lights were merely suggestions.

And the "beautiful" city of Huế was a dump.

And how did this country operate when whole teams of "repairmen" couldn't figure out that our recalcitrant air conditioner merely needed a shot of Freon?

Maybe we couldn't do this after all—maybe we were just too old. Maybe we just weren't cut out to be expatriates.

Release

I hesitantly picked up the phone and called Peter. Though Peter was in Hà Nội and was much younger than we were, he was an experienced teacher in Việt Nam. Our teaching agency had wisely set up a system of the experienced people mentoring the newbies.

Peter (chuckling on the phone): "Yeah—you're right on schedule!"

Me (mildly upset and angry): "Whaddya mean, 'We're right on schedule'"?

Peter: "You've been here about six weeks, right? Do you remember your training? You are hitting the culture shock wall, my friend."

And truthfully—I had forgotten my training. They had told us all about culture shock, but during my angry moments, I had forgotten all that good knowledge.

Peter: "Doug—just up Lê Lợi Street—right on the river—is the Century Hotel."

Me: "Yeah—so what?"

Peter: "So take tomorrow off, go on up to the hotel, and for two bucks, they will let you into the big pool there. Western people—Western food—a little luxury. A mini-vacation."

Me: "We can't do that! We have lesson plans to write and things to plan! We can't do that!"

Peter: "Oh yes, you can. You've been teaching for six weeks—you know what to do in class. Besides—be a little bit Vietnamese and don't plan so much. I'll fly down to Huế in a few days and check on you guys. But really—you're as normal as can be—right on schedule."

And thus it was—though we never did go swimming at the Century Hotel, we knew we were going to be okay. Cindy had given herself permission to go home—and found she didn't need to. And I let go of my anger—and my superiority complex. Not only did I no longer have to assume my husbandly duties of protecting my wife from the new culture, but I began to look on my recent behavior sheepishly. I had been ugly and rude. I had been over-the-top in my judgmentalism. I had indeed expected Việt Nam to change just because Doug Young had arrived.

The peak of the fever had passed. We had hit the culture shock wall and survived.

Good morning, Việt Nam!

We felt at home, and now we could start to learn more about our new home. Where we had once only seen Huế as ugly and shabby, we now looked past the mold and peeling paint—and we saw a beautiful city worthy of its reputation.

As the strain of writing lesson plans, teaching classes, and learning our way around the city began to lessen, we had more time. Life became fun again—like it had been in the first few weeks, only we now had the confidence to explore.

Our bicycles gave us freedom—we could get around town to see more of the city and its people.

Getting to Know You

It's easy to observe Vietnamese society from a bicycle, because life is still largely lived outside. The people are outside because air conditioning has yet to keep everyone inside—no air-conditioned cars, stores, classrooms, and homes, as in America.

While out and about on my bicycle, hunger might strike. Not a problem. "Street food" can be found at any time, night or day. In the morning, the soup ladies are ready with a quick breakfast. Phở is beef noodle soup with a kick—one could say it is the national dish of Việt Nam. Near the university campus, there were students coming to class in the morning in need of a quick, nourishing, and inexpensive breakfast. Soup fits the bill nicely. The vendors bring the food, the dishes, and the little stools for customers along with them, carrying everything in two baskets suspended by a bamboo pole perched on a shoulder. They even bring the fire for heating the soup. The vendors' morning ends at about eight thirty, when all the students are in class.

I've never been an early riser, except when the army made me arise early. But in Huế, morning classes started at 7:00 a.m. There were more than a few days when I got up just in time to get dressed, slug down a cup of coffee, and get out the door. That's when I discovered sticky rice.

Little old ladies can easily be found selling balls of sticky rice—usually with some sort of other food mixed within, such as beans or pork. Often it is sold wrapped in a banana leaf. I didn't need to speak Vietnamese to order one—street food vendors only sell one product—there is no menu to select from. I could ride to my classroom, stop and buy a ball of sticky rice, and eat it before getting to class. Very cheap—very filling—and very nourishing.

Cindy was not as explorative about "street food" as I was, but not because of any antipathy to Vietnamese food—it's just that she is a nurse, and nurses have this thing about everything being perfectly sanitary. But I never got sick from eating street food—except for the time I ate bun hen (say *boon hen*), white noodles, and bean sprouts, with some of the local river mussels mixed in with some greens. It is a local Huế specialty, and is very spicy. Even my students had warned me about eating bun hen—one's stomach has to be accustomed to the river water. I should have known better—despite its romantic name, the Perfume River is badly polluted, and any mussels from the river were bound to be nasty. I never suffered anything more than a queasy stomach that one time.

Students at the nearby Đại Học Sư Phạm (Teacher's College) can get a quick breakfast of rice, soup, or noodles before classes begin at 7:00 a.m. The vendors set up shop before dawn, then pack up and leave by 8:30 a.m. or so.

I had a third-year writing student named Nhân (say *nyun*) whom I asked to work with me. He was from the city of Nha Trang (say *Nyah Trang*)—not a Huế native—so Huế was a different place for him too. I would get curious about something, and I'd ask Nhân to translate.

"Mr. Doug—maybe you should say something in Vietnamese too. The people like to hear a Westerner try to speak Vietnamese. They think you are courteous if you do."

That made a lot of sense to me. "*Chào anh*," I'd chirp to a man about my age, or "*Chào bà,*" to an older lady. Often I'd see a puzzled expression, but after they had sifted through my thick accent, the smile would appear, and they'd answer me in a torrent of Vietnamese. Nhân was quick to explain that I'd said all the Vietnamese I knew—but that was enough. People were willing to share stories with the old foreigner, and I'd take out my camera with a smile.

And they would talk to me. One woman told me she was unmarried, and I guessed she was in her mid-thirties. She lived with her parents, and sold food to make a little extra income for the household. Her day began at 5:00 a.m. Her specialty was bún bò Huế (say *boon baw hway*), a spicy noodle soup.

No foreigners bought her fare, but the shop owners appreciated quick, hearty, and cheap food, brought right to the doorstep. Her equipment included a large pot of hot broth with a small fire under it. She only charged 1,000 Vietnamese Đồng (pronounced *dome* and abbreviated VND; at that time the conversion rate was 15,000 Đồng to the U.S. dollar). She felt she'd had a good day if her profit was between 10,000 and 15,000 VND—a dollar a day.

Street vendors have not shared in the growth of the economy. Most are poorly educated, and have no other way to make a living. Worse, as consumers have more money, they often opt to eat in a restaurant. But street vendors are still a fixture of Vietnamese life, and probably will be for some time.

I saw both men and women selling food, but it seems men sold food only if there was another means of conveyance than a shoulder pole and baskets—that was a woman's way of carrying things. One male vendor had a bicycle with a contraption on the back that held a small fire. He sold bánh bao (say *bahn bow*, as in bow wow)—sweet tasting bread stuffed with other food. It could be meat or vegetarian bánh bao. Huế is considered the center of Buddhism in Việt Nam, and Buddhist monks are vegetarians. Some of the more ardent believers are vegetarians too. Vegetarian bánh bao is popular during the periods within the lunar month when many Buddhists observe stricter dietary rules.

As expected, the men are more aggressive sellers than the women. One vendor was quite proud of his bánh bao, charging 5,000 VND—about thirty-three cents. Maybe he charged me extra because I was a foreigner. Though the practice of asking more money from tourists is disappearing slowly, foreigners are often charged more than Vietnamese for the same article or service. But the newer stores have bar code readers—no bargaining allowed. Foreigners, friends of the owner, or newcomers pay the same price.

When I was a kid, I played stick ball in the street—well, mostly in the street. Third base might be on the left sidewalk. If the ball was hit hard, it might be shorter to chase it on the sidewalk, rather than try to maneuver past the old Buick parked on the street. If you live in the American suburbs, live in the city, or live in a small town, you are familiar with sidewalks. You see sidewalks in residential neighborhoods and downtown areas. We're pretty used to them in America, even if we don't use them all that much in the suburbs. They're used more in the city, to get from the office to the sandwich shop.

Her day began at 3:00 a.m. She arose in her little one-room home with a dirt floor and thatched roof. She has no husband to feed, no children, and no other family. The broth had been simmering since the previous evening, and she prepared the noodles in the morning. At 4:00 a.m., she began the walk from her village of Nhât Dông, into the city—a distance of 6 kilometers (about 3.7 miles).

Chewing some betel nut helped the walk seem shorter. She stayed in Huế until her food either sold out, or until lunch hour. She may have eaten her remaining food for lunch, then, as per Vietnamese custom, she took a nap during the heat of the day. She then went by an open-air market to buy the ingredients for the next day's batch of bún bò Huế.

But for the most part, sidewalks are not an integral part of social life in North America.

Not so in Việt Nam. Sidewalks are a huge part of the public fiber of any city or town. Everything is done on the sidewalk—food is sold and consumed on the sidewalk. Motorbikes are repaired and parked on the sidewalk. Vendors hawk their wares on the sidewalk. Enclosed stores open out to the sidewalk—and probably have a rack or display out on the sidewalk. People use the sidewalk for just about everything except walking. Sidewalks blend with the street. Sometimes you don't know if you should be walking on the sidewalk or the street.

And the sidewalk is where bicycle repairmen do business. There is almost always something wrong with an inexpensive Vietnamese bicycle, but this lack of reliability provides employment for legions of repairmen. Their advertisement is usually two old tires tied together.

Life is hard on these bikemen. They work with the most basic of tools. The nut that joins the handlebars to the front wheel came loose on my bike. The bikeman didn't have an Allen wrench the right size, so he just pounded the closest size he had into the nut, and made it work. The bikeman must be ready to carry his "shop" with him whenever he needs to go home, so everything he owns is carried in some simple containers.

You can eat on the street, and you can get your bicycle fixed on the street—but the street can obviously take you places such as markets, post offices, stores, and restaurants.

In the big cities, there are lots of enclosed restaurants with air conditioning, and the smaller cities are starting to see upscale restaurants too, but these are usually for tourists. Most eateries open right on to the street.

As I mentioned above, phở is my favorite food. After Việt Nam's reunification in 1975, the Communist government banned phở as a bourgeois luxury, but once the country began to open up again in the late 1980s, phở places sprouted quickly. It is noodle soup, made with a rich beef stock that includes bone marrow. There are different styles—the style favored in the south is Sài Gòn style—served with lime, lots of herbs (I call it shrubbery), bean sprouts, and pepper sauce added to your taste. The northern version is more austere.

The Phở Sài Gòn restaurant became our favorite place to eat. The owner soon got to know us as she practiced her English at our table. A good businesswoman, by the time we left Việt Nam, she had opened a second restaurant in Đa Nẵng.

I also learned a lesson in Vietnamese culture at Phở Sài Gòn. I learned the value of relationships.
No—I don't mean people are nice to you because you are a Westerner, nor do I mean people are nice because they are trying to get money. I mean that if you take the time to get to know someone—if you take the time to build relationships—you will come to know the culture in a deeper way.

Not long after I traded up from a bicycle to a motorbike, we were eating at Phở Sài Gòn. We paid for our meal and began to leave, only to find I had a flat tire. A bicycle repairman could have fixed the tire, but it was too late in the evening, and they had all gone home.

Old American ammunition cans left over from the war are prized by the bicycle repairmen, because they are rugged and waterproof. The can with no lid has water in it, which is used to find inner tube leaks. The others hold tools.

Above: Shoe vendors and other street sellers often must pay a little extra to the police, to set up on the sidewalks. While food vendors still flourish on the streets, merchandise peddlers such as this man are disappearing, as newer chain stores appear.

Below: Different foods are available at different times. Fresh boiled corn can be had at night. Government food inspection has yet to arrive for the street vendors. While many tourist guidebooks eschew "street food," I ate it frequently, with no ill effects.

Huế is the foodie center of Việt Nam. The locals will tell you that's because it was the last imperial capital of the country—the local food was made for a king. Many dishes were in fact developed and served to the king, and those recipes survive today.

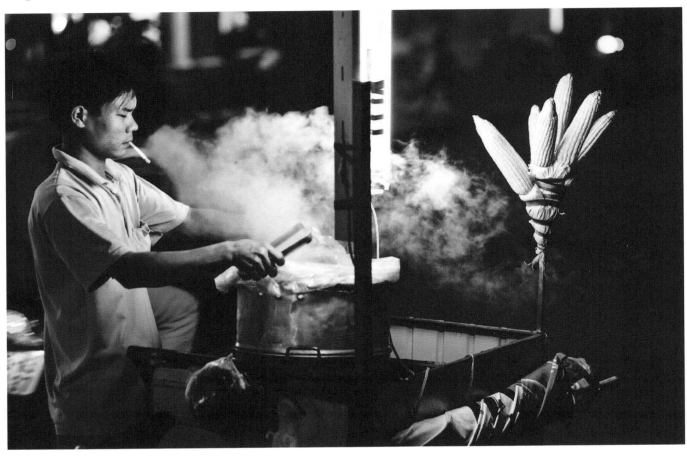

It was raining, and we were on the other side of town from our apartment. What to do?

Phở Sài Gòn's owner to the rescue. In her fractured English, she told me to park the motorbike inside the restaurant for the night, and go home in a taxi. In the morning I could return, get the motorbike, and then walk it two blocks to the Honda dealership. I had taken the time to know her, helped her practice her English—and she helped me.

Years after that experience, whenever we return to Huế and a bowl of phở, we always take time to talk to her—and to notice that the photo I took of her and the restaurant still hangs on the wall near the cash drawer.

When I say the Vietnamese culture is relationship-based, I'm not kidding. Westerners are so task-oriented; we keep "relationships" as a separate part of our lives. To the Vietnamese, relationships are central. To Americans, personal relationships get in the way of business. To the Vietnamese, they don't know how to do business unless it is within a relationship. For Americans, it is nepotism or a conflict of interest—the Vietnamese do business with family and friends first, because they can be trusted.

Food vendors vary according to the time of day—different foods sold at different times—but the bicycle repairmen work from before dawn until after dusk. These men make very little money, and as the economy improves and more people buy motorbikes and automobiles, the demand for bicycle repair will continue to decline.

Note the two bicycle tires tied together. They are the repairmen's advertising. The bikemen set up "shop" on a busy street corner, and then hope the police will leave them alone and they will get some business.

This conversation took place between our teaching teammate, Julie Louis (who spoke fluent Vietnamese), and a lady at the neighborhood market.

Julie: "Hello, older sister! How's your health?"

Grocer: "Hello, younger sister. I'm fine, and you?"

Julie: "Good."

Grocer: "Aren't you cold? You aren't wearing a jacket."

Julie: "No, I'm okay because I get warm, pedaling my bike."

What few child labor laws that exist are seldom enforced, but restaurant work is good work for girls.

Grocer: "What would you like?"

Julie: "Two kilos of apples."

Grocer: "Why do you want so many?"

Julie: "My friend didn't buy enough when she came here this morning. We're going to make a special American pie for a holiday we're celebrating today, called Thanksgiving."

Grocer: "That American was your friend? Oh, I'm so sorry! I didn't know. I charged her so much! I shouldn't have done that. I promise I will give her a good price next time. I'm so sorry." (As she grabs onto Julie and buries her face in her sleeve)

Julie: "It's okay, don't worry about it. How much do I owe you?"

Grocer: "Twenty-five thousand Đông." (less than two dollars)

Julie: "Thanks, older sister."

The end of the day, the customers gone, as Cindy and Tuan enjoy a late evening conversation at the Phở Sài Gòn restaurant. Tuan went on to attend the University of Texas at San Antonio, for his doctorate in environmental science.

Grocer: "Goodbye."

You're wondering, "What's this 'older sister' stuff?" The answer is your first clue about how important relationships are in Việt Nam.

Personal pronouns in the Vietnamese language are based on how old the other person is in relation to you. In this case, Julie is younger than the grocer, therefore Julie uses the word *chi* (older sister) when addressing the grocer. The grocer called Julie *em*, an affectionate diminutive used when talking to younger people. (Em is also a cozy word a boy calls his girlfriend. Think of how the word "baby" is used in American slang.)

Put another way, there is no way to say "How are you today?" simply because there is no word for "you." To talk to another person, you must have a relationship, even if it is nothing more than knowing whether the other person is older than you.

Of course, the grocer was referring to Cindy when she spoke of "that American." Foreigners often think the Vietnamese are always out to rip them off. Not always so—they trade on the basis of relationships. Julie has taken the time to know the grocer, and is treated accordingly. The next time Cindy goes there, she too will be treated like a friend.

Now imagine Julie at the Đông Ba (say *Dome Bah*) market, and she's going into a new shop where she doesn't know the seller. She's chosen what she wants to buy, and goes to the shop keeper to pay for it. This is how the conversation is likely to transpire:

Julie: "Hello."

Seller: "Hello. Where are you from?" (As she takes Julie's goods to determine the price)

Julie: "America."

Seller: "How old are you?"

Julie: "Twenty-seven."

Seller: "Do you have a family yet?"

Julie: "Not yet."

Seller: "Do you have a boyfriend yet?"

Julie: "Yes."

Seller: "When will you get married?"

Julie: "I don't know yet; maybe next year."

Seller: (putting Julie's goods in a plastic bag) "You speak Vietnamese very well… Nine thousand Đông."

Julie: (handing the seller the money and taking the bag) "Thank you."

Can you imagine having a conversation like that the next time you go to Home Depot or Wal-Mart? You will be lucky if the clerk looks at you, much less engages you in conversation. Most likely, you would be very offended if a clerk asked your marital status. In this conversation, if Julie had said she did not have a man in her life, the clerk would probably have admonished her to find a boyfriend, get married, and have children. If the clerk at Wal-Mart told you to get married, you'd probably report her to the manager.

In Việt Nam, it's all about relationships.

But for me, the big Đông Ba market was not a good place to learn about relationships. For me, it wasn't even a good place to buy anything. I hated the place.

I have big feet, even by American standards. One thing I had forgotten to bring to Việt Nam was a pair of rubber sandals—the kind of flip-flops worn at the beach. In my case, I needed a pair to wear around our apartment. We had quickly adopted the Vietnamese custom of taking off our street shoes when entering the apartment, simply because the rainy season of Huế made our shoes filthy. Kick off the shoes at the door, and slip on some flip-flops. But I didn't have any flip-flops to wear, and the tile floor was hard on my old feet.

Off to Đông Ba market to try to find some rubber sandals. Đông Ba is the big central marketplace in Huế. There are lots of other smaller markets, but Đông Ba is by far the largest. We didn't really know our way around the city yet—all we knew was Đông Ba. At this early stage of our life in Huế, just crossing the bridge over the Perfume River to get to the Đông Ba Market was a major adventure.

And it is packed solid with people, most of whom are talking very loudly. Like most Westerners, I have a sense of "personal space." Don't crowd me. I don't like people bumping against me. I don't like the feel of other people's sweatiness on me.

I really didn't like being in the Đông Ba market.

The Vietnamese have no such sense of personal space. Rather than stand in nice, neat lines to wait for something, they would rather bunch into a large crowd. They're not bothered at all by large packs of people. Pushing and shoving is normal behavior. It's not considered impolite. It was another lesson to be learned in a new culture—the Vietnamese don't have a problem with crowds.

And Đông Ba was definitely crowded. Lots of people shoving and pushing—and very annoying to me. The noise levels were louder than a rock concert as vendors, shoppers and xích lô drivers yelled to be heard above the din. But we were at the market to find some flip-flops for me, so we plunged into the mass of people.

There were lots of shoe vendors, many of them tugging at my sleeves to direct me toward their stall. But once the vendors saw the size of my feet, they just laughed. I'll guess that few Vietnamese men have shoes larger than a size eight, and my size twelves were way out of range.

I couldn't really "shop" at Đông Ba. (To be honest, I really don't like to shop anyway—even in America.) The noise and the crowds totally distracted me. There was no way I was going to establish a relationship with anyone in the Đông Ba market, least of all with a vendor who was pushing shoes under my nose in an annoying attempt to get me to buy something I didn't need.

As time passed, Cindy returned to Đông Ba many times, but I continued to stay away from the place as much as I could.

The rural village open-air markets were good places for me to see relationships at work.

I met Cu at the Mandarin at half-past ridiculous in the morning. We downed some eggs, bacon, and coffee, then each threw a leg over our motorbikes and rode north out of the city. Though it was still dark, many Vietnamese were up and about, and the streets were starting to get busy. Cu knew I liked to shoot pictures of rural markets, and he knew we needed to be there before the people arrived. Cu enjoyed our little photo outings, but the trips were part of his business too. The Mandarin Café does a sizable business selling Cu's excellent photos of the people around Huế.

The Đông Ba market is built in two parts - the large two-story indoor building is for clothing, jewelry, shoes and other durable goods. It's where tourists go to buy souvenirs. That was the place I disliked. The outside market was very different, though still noisy. It was crowded too, but not jammed elbow-to-elbow as is the indoor market. I loved the outdoor market. It's where food is sold: vegetables, fish, fruit, and meat.

I am sometimes asked how I survived living in Việt Nam without being able to speak the language. It was not difficult, using the magic of a smile, gestures, and a willingness to laugh at oneself. The LCD display on the back of a digital camera works wonders.

Photo courtesy Phan Cu

The market in Quảng An commune northeast of Huế was like many others in the small villages of central Việt Nam. The sun wasn't fully up, and the waterways were still misty when the first vendors begin arriving. Sellers came from the surrounding countryside by boat, bicycle, foot, and motorbike. Cu and I joined others as we parked and locked our motorbikes, and walked down an embankment to the village.

Soon the place was noisy, packed, and exciting. Noisy because the women were loud as they argued over prices, buyers denigrated the products as they bargained for a lower price, and everyone exchanged the news of the day. The "seafood section" of the market offered fin fish, squid, shrimp, shellfish—it was all there. Not only could you find what you wanted, but it didn't get any fresher than "still wigglin' in the basket."

Maybe a housewife had a hankering for pork. No problem. The pig was alive only a few hours ago, and the meat was fresh. Some deft work with a big knife quickly reduced him to edible pieces. About an hour after her first sale, the pork dealer was almost sold out.

The Vietnamese diet doesn't include a lot of meat. It's a very healthy diet of fresh vegetables—lots of soups—with protein and flavoring coming from seafood, chicken, pork, and a little beef.

The traditional Vietnamese market is a contradiction. When most Western tourists see an open-air market such as the large Đông Ba market in Huế (left), they think of bad sanitation and health problems. The large majority of Vietnamese who live in the smaller cities or countryside do not have a refrigerator at home, so they make daily (often twice daily) trips to the market. As a result, the turnover of food is fast—nothing stays out in the sun to spoil— and food is fresh.

Because women come to the market frequently, they build deep relationships with their neighbors. This is the place where the news of the day is spread, and gossip is exchanged.

Many of the market sellers will also carry their baskets of food into the city, to hawk their wares up and down the streets. For the elderly and infirm, it is a way to continue to get the local news when the vendors stop by their homes.

Việt Nam is still primarily an outdoor culture, but that will change as more people have air conditioning, automobiles, and televisions to help people isolate themselves from their neighbors.

The buyers and vendors alike may have a bowl of soup in their hands. If you've ever munched on a candy bar while shopping in America, then you know that busy people shop and eat at the same time. A good entrepreneur will see the business potential, and sell prepared food to shoppers whether in the United States or in Việt Nam.

There were a number of places in the market to buy prepared food, including a soup stall. You could get a quick order if you wished, and either eat it at the stall or take it as carry-out.

Business in the market was brisk. From eggs to squid, a lot of women did a lot of buying and selling in a short period of time. There were a few men around, including a one-legged elderly gentleman who collected the rent money from the vendors, but most of the men were hangers-on. Women ran the place.

Though the vast majority of the people in the market are women, this one-legged man functions as the market master, collecting the minuscule rent monies that go to the village coffers. He was once a soldier in the southern army, and lost his leg in the disastrous Operation Lam Son 719 of 1971.

There were a lot of kids around the market. They weren't playing hooky from school—they went in the afternoon. School was in session all day, except for lunch and nap time, Monday through Saturday, with half of the children attending in the morning and half in the afternoon.

As mid-morning approached, the market crowd thinned out; the vendors packed away their scales, baskets, and other paraphernalia, and the area became quiet again.

Above: Mom is busy selling vegetables in the market, but still keeps an eye on her child. In the villages, where the traditional Vietnamese culture still thrives, the child will be safe, and any mother is expected to discipline or help any child not her own.

Top: A wide variety of seafood is available in the central parts of Việt Nam, due to proximity to the ocean. Note the empty bowl in the buyer's hands—she just finished a bowl of soup on the go.

Above: Chicken and pork are the two main sources of meat in the Vietnamese diet. This pig was slaughtered before dawn, the blood drained, and the meat brought to market for sale. The seller will gladly give the buyer a custom cut.

Following pages:

What these old eyes have seen.

She has seen two wars herself, and probably sent sons off to fight in a third in Cambodia. She has toiled in the rice fields, raised children, and kept the house. Her life has been very hard.

Yet she smiles.

Living in Việt Nam and meeting people such as this wonderful lady changed me. Even today, as I look at this photo hanging on the wall of my home, I look into her eyes, and she seems to be telling me that there is more to life than the acquisition of things.

Her home is a simple stucco-covered brick house with the traditional three rooms and a family altar for worshiping her ancestors. There is a television for the younger people to watch. She has no cell phone, though her children have one. She has no motorbike, though her grandson takes her to market on one. Her life now is to keep the house clean for the rest of the family, and to do some cooking. She is doted on by the other three generations in the house.

And she is happy.

The ladies walked home with their purchases, and the world awaited tomorrow's dawn and another day for the village market.

The countryside is where I find the "real" Việt Nam. Of course, the cities are real too, but I always love getting on my motorbike and riding out to the small villages—going places few tourists go. For some travelers, after making a three-week visit, they feel qualified to go home and write a book about the country, but I found that the longer I lived in Việt Nam, the less I seemed to really know about it.

And I wanted to know all I could about the country and its people.

As we grew in our knowledge and love of the country, we stayed in touch with people back home, trying to help them understand how similar, yet how different, life was in Việt Nam—how much we were learning—and how much we wanted to learn. We blogged and e-mailed, and generally put the Internet to good use.

I tried to pay extra attention to my mother. While other people could read my blog postings or share the photos I posted on the Web, Mom was typical of her generation in not having a lot of technical savvy. She had a computer, and knew how to receive and send e-mails, but she much preferred paper letters. They were something she could hold in her hand and show her friends at church. Cindy and I made it a point to send our mothers regular printed letters, written in larger typeface, and with the pictures on the paper. We tried to make them newsy and personal. Cindy's father had died in 2004, just before we left—both of our mothers were widows. It mattered to neither mother that it took two weeks or so for the letters to arrive from Việt Nam—as long as they heard from their children, and knew they were safe and happy.

Our letters were chatty. Mom was approaching ninety, and was in the early stages of Alzheimer's when we left. Keeping things simple and including lots of photos was what she needed.

I had been good about keeping people back home informed during the war too.

I was newsy in 1969 too—but I probably shouldn't have been. As I read these letters now, I wonder how much anguish I caused. A mother does not need to know that her son was involved in combat operations where five men died and twenty three were wounded.

If my mother ever felt any angst at reading my letters, she never said so. I found my letters to her many years later. I have none of the letters she sent me—we were instructed to burn our letters from home, lest the enemy find them and send nasty notes to our families.

My letters to her were short—very short. We didn't have much time for letter writing. The 1st Cavalry Division was the original helicopter unit—we made a heli-borne assault every three days—more if the tactical situation warranted. The normal cycle was to spend fifteen days in the jungle, followed by five days on the sandbagged jungle outpost we called a landing zone—or LZ, for short.

Out in the field, we had to carry everything on our backs. In addition to our weapons and ammunition, food and water for three days, and items such as batteries for our radios, even small items such as a pad of paper and pen were just too much to carry. Besides, we moved during the daytime, and had no time to write. At night, we circled up in a defensive position or set out ambushes. Obviously, no lights were allowed after dark. Our five days back on the LZ were the only time we had for connecting with home.

COMPANY "C"
2nd BATTALION 5th CAVALRY
1st CAVALRY DIVISION (AM)
APO SAN FRANCISCO 96490

Dear Mom & Russ –

I guess it's about time I wrote a letter. We are
on the LZ now, and I am hiding so I can find some time
to write. I just wrote Judy a letter – for the first
time in 2½ weeks, so you can see how bad things are.

As you have read in the papers, Tay Ninh is very
bad right now. We just came off 15 days in the field,
during which time we had 6 dead and 23 wounded.
So as you can see, there's a war on. And even
though they are pulling troops out, it will be a long
time before this war is over.

Well, sounds to me like you are quite busy again.
What kind of a job does Russ have? You never did
explain it in your letter. And it sounds as if you are
progressing quite well in the J.C. Penny Co. But
just as before, don't overburden yourself with too

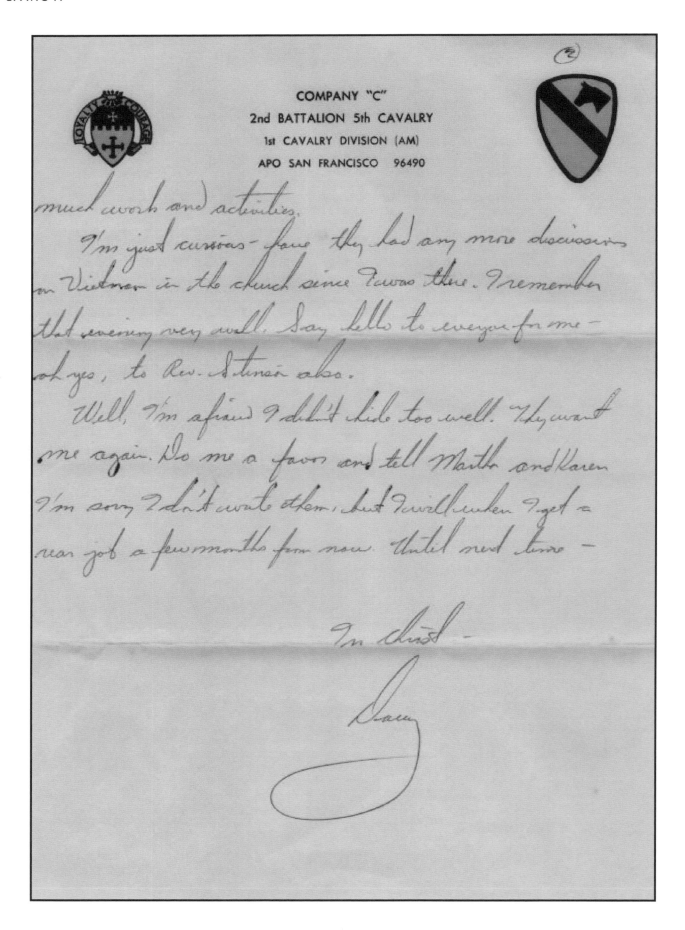

COMPANY "C"
2nd BATTALION 5th CAVALRY
1st CAVALRY DIVISION (AM)
APO SAN FRANCISCO 96490

much work and activities.

I'm just curious - have they had any more discussions on Vietnam in the church since I was there. I remember that evening very well. Say hello to everyone for me - oh yes, to Rev. Stinson also.

Well, I'm afraid I didn't hide too well. They want me again. Do me a favor and tell Martha and Karen I'm sorry I don't write them, but I will when I get a rear job a few months from now. Until next time -

In Christ -

Gary

By the second semester, we had a very comfortable, nicely furnished two-room apartment on the second floor.

The guest house was built with funds from the East Meets West Foundation, a charitable organization founded by Le Ly Hayslip, a refugee from Đa Nẵng who became wealthy in America. Her story was chronicled in the book, "When Heaven and Earth Changed Places," and later in a movie of the same name by Oliver Stone. East Meets West also built Huế University's library.

By the beginning of the fall semester of 2005, we had new digs. We moved into a guest house in the Vỹ Dạ (say *Vee Yah*) section of Huế. We were outside the central part of the city—and well away from our classrooms. Bicycles weren't going to hack it for us two old people in the Vietnamese heat.

It was time to buy a motorbike for me, and an electric bicycle for Cindy.

Being a law-abiding person, I also needed to get a Vietnamese driver's license. I knew that the police seldom stop foreigners, because few police officers speak English, and also because they don't want to irritate tourists. But, I wanted to do it the right way.

And in so doing, I got another taste of the Vietnamese bureaucracy. I had my American driver's license translated, which allowed me to bypass taking the written exam, but I still had to take the driving portion of the exam. That meant riding a motorbike in a proscribed figure eight without letting my feet touch the ground.

Harder than it might seem.

I practiced and practiced, but when the day came to take the test, I blew it. Though I finished the figure eight, my foot had touched the ground, and I knew I would not get my license that day.

Then I looked at the table where the examiners sat, and saw the young lady who had come to translate for me talking to them.

Our motorbike was a Honda Dream—think of it as a utilitarian minivan. The little 110cc engine was geared very low, which allowed two hefty Americans to keep up with city traffic with ease. While we lived in Huế, there was no law requiring helmet use, but we wore them anyway. Since then, Việt Nam has enacted a helmet law to help lower the very high traffic accident mortality rate.

Mr. Cu helped me take delivery of the motorbike on my birthday in October, 2006. I paid $1,100 for it, then sold it the following June, when we returned to the United States, for $800. Having daily transportation for $300 over eight months was pretty good.

Cindy's electric bicycle was perfect for her to get to class and to run errands. When we went out for dinner at night, we packed double on the motorbike, rain or shine.

Photo courtesy Phan Cu

Thao Hien (say *Tah-oh Hee-in*) pointed at me with her beatific smile, turned back to the table, and said something. The official looked at me, nodded—then pulled out his red stamp and approved my license.

"Thao Hien—what did you say to him? You know I failed."

"I just said that the old man had practiced so hard, and that you were in Việt Nam to teach."

The old man got his driver's license.

Buying the motorbike gave me another insight into the Vietnamese culture. Unlike Americans, the Vietnamese have no hesitation talking about money and how much you have paid for an item—especially a relatively expensive item like a motorbike. I got my first taste of this phenomenon as I parked my new moto in front of the Mandarin Café.

Xích lô driver who hung around the Mandarin: "Hey, Mr. Dough. Your motorbike? How much you pay?"[6]

Phương, a waitress at the Mandarin: "Ooooh! Can I ride it? Mistah Cu help you buy? How much you pay?"

First year male student: "Ah, Teacher—you bought a motorbike. Very nice. You buy new? How much Đông you pay?"

The questions lasted about three days, until the newness of my acquisition wore off. I was intrigued that people living in a country whose per capita income is $1,052 per year talked so easily about money, yet my own culture's obsession with buying expensive cars as an expression of wealth makes it taboo to talk about money.

But we hadn't traveled to the other side of the world for some sort of cultural exchange—we were in Việt Nam to be teachers—specifically, to be English teachers at the University of Huế. We were not "guest" teachers either—we were members of the faculty in the English Department of the College of Foreign Languages. Our contract called for us to be paid the same as a new Vietnamese teacher would be paid (about $45 a month at that time), and for the college to provide housing. For that, we taught twelve to sixteen hours per week.

And we loved it.

More correctly, we loved it once we got used to the differences between the Western system we grew up with and the Vietnamese system.

In the American high school system, the teacher stays in the same room, and the students move between classrooms. The American higher education system is similar, except that most professors don't teach all day, so the same classroom may be used by a few different teachers. It is quite the opposite in Việt Nam— the students stay in the same classroom, while the teachers move from room to room.

---

6 Even well-educated Vietnamese often mispronounce my name. They were taught that an "h" should follow a "g" at the end of a word. Even after being corrected, most have difficulty pronouncing my name, as there is no word that ends with the "g" sound in Vietnamese. I was either "Mr. Dough" or "Mr. Duck."

Students in a first-year (freshman) speaking class are split into small groups to practice a conversational speaking assignment I had given them. Later, each group was asked to come to the front of the room. All my students were English majors. Note that most of them are female.

We did not have to know Vietnamese, because all our students spoke English. Our job was to help them polish their skills.

Electives—no such thing in the Vietnamese system while we were there. The curriculum was set, and students had no way of taking any other courses.[7]

Most English majors are girls.[8] All students have taken English in high school, and have passed very competitive university entrance exams before being admitted to the English department. But that does not necessarily mean they can speak or write English. It means they have studied the grammar and syntax of English, but have not always learned how to use the language. That's where native speaking English teach-

7 This is changing as Vietnamese universities move to the kind of credit hour system used in the west. Much is changing, and changing very quickly. When we arrived in the spring term of 2005, desks were of the type seen in old Western movies—seat and desk for two as one unit, and bolted to the floor. By the next year, those were removed, and folding student desks were in the classroom, which allowed teachers to break students into small groups for practical exercises and group study.
8 Your marital status determines whether you are a girl or a woman in Việt Nam, not your age. I questioned one of my third-year classes about this, and the ladies were very vocal about wanting to be referred to as girls. To be a woman means you are married, but if you are single, yet addressed as a woman, then the inference could be made that you are sexually active, and that is not acceptable in conservative Huế.

ers come in. We can help the students pronounce English correctly, and teach the many idioms and nuances used in everyday English. In other words, we taught them how to communicate in English, building on the skills they had already learned in high school.

I met with my first-year speaking class twice each week—two hours each time. There were sixty students in the class. That is not a typo—I had sixty students. They were chatty, noisy, and fun- loving. When I first started with this group in the fall of 2005, they were disconcerted by the fact that I often arrived in the classroom before they did. Normally, the Vietnamese teachers arrive after the students, who stand up when the teacher enters the room. But as a typical American, I usually got to class a little early so I could have my material ready. The class slowly got used to me, and after a while, didn't pay much attention when I entered, other than a polite, "Good afternoon, Teacher."

Vietnamese students have attended school in a culture long dominated by Confucian ideals. When Việt Nam was ruled by kings, only the king received a higher level of respect than a teacher. To the student, the teacher is an expert, and not to be questioned. While it was nice to be highly respected, this respect also results in very passive students. Students were used to being told what to learn, and interaction in the classroom was seldom done. In Việt Nam, traditional teachers do not ask questions, and most certainly a student would not ask the teacher a question, as that might impugn the teacher's knowledge, and cause him/her to lose face.

Because I was a Westerner, the school encouraged me to use Western teaching methodologies, which usu-ally involves lots of interactivity. I could not be interactive in the classroom if the students were passive, so I had to get them up and moving. On one occasion, after we had exchanged "beginning of class pleasantries," I had them count off by twos—then we walked down three flights of steps to the courtyard. All the "Ones" lined up on the left, and all the "Twos" lined up on the right. We did some role playing, with the "Ones" pretending to be British tourists looking for a good restaurant, and the "Twos" recommending a place and giving directions for how to get to the restaurant. During the exercise, I peeked up at the second floor bal-cony to see a Vietnamese teacher scowling his disapproval.

The exercise got 'em moving and talking. Now they were ready to do some active learning, so I sent them back upstairs in new groups of four. I had another exercise designed to do two things—to practice English among themselves, and to develop their own learning strategies. Each group was to come up with some ideas for practicing English out of class. After working for a few minutes, a few students stood up and told the rest of the class their group's ideas. Of course, I selected the member of the group who would stand up and make the report—that made all of them work on the project. This was a noisy time in the classroom (and I sometimes wonder if we were upsetting the surrounding classrooms, as there was no air conditioning and the windows were open), but they were practicing normal conversation and increasing their vocabulary.

Problem solving is an important part of learning. I seldom gave students a direct answer to their questions, and I often gave them some sort of puzzle to solve. The traditional Vietnamese educator just gives facts. As a country, Việt Nam knows it will have to change its educational system in order to compete in the world. It now has a well educated work force that attracts businesses for its skill and low wages, but business leaders must possess higher level thinking skills if Việt Nam is to stay on its current rapid course of economic expansion.

During my second semester, I exchanged e-mails with a student. She described herself as very shy, but wanted to thank me for giving her confidence in her ability to speak English. I continued to encourage her, and she eventually volunteered to write something about Việt Nam. I asked her to write about her daily life as a first-year university student. She did—and here is what she wrote. I have not edited it one little bit.

I'm happy that you want to know about Viet Nam student'life. In addition, the life of VN student is very different. The students whose parent are rich, have a very good life, but the others who are poor have many dificulties in their lives. However, they are very happy and interested in student life. To me, I'm a poor student, so my life is also hard. My mother is a nurse, my father is retired. I have a brother studying in Agriculture and Forestry University. It's difficult for my mother to provide money for me and my brother. Now we are going to cook ourselves because it's cheaper and more convenient than I eat at anywhere else. Everyday I often have breakfast with loaf and milk (it costs me 3000 VN DONG!). I usually go to market for lunch and also for dinner. Vegetable is my favorite food,but price is expensive. I often cook a meal for lunch and for dinner. Although my meal is not really good, I' ll try to get over any difficulty to study. I hope you can understand what I say. ...it takes me 1 hour to write and send this mail. I like it very much.

How could I not love teaching students like that?

Students pretend they are calling me on the telephone after they have learned I am sick. The fun part is when I "talk" to one of them on the "phone," and say something they do not expect.

Contrary to American ways, when a person gets sick in Việt Nam, he or she can expect all his friends to call and visit. We Westerners feel we need to be left alone so we can rest, but it would be very insulting to a Vietnamese to be left alone while sick.

English majors had to take a semester of British Culture and a semester of American Culture. When I first arrived at the university, I was assigned to teach a big combined section of two classes—I was supposed to have one section, and Mr. Dương Lâm Anh the other, but he had a serious back problem that made it difficult to stand for any period of time. Once a week, I would go to Lâm Anh's house, and we'd talk about the next class session. We would pull out the textbook he had compiled—and we'd talk. He'd done graduate work in Boston, and his area of interest was American culture. He proved to be a good observer of America.

Lâm Anh: "Next chapter in the textbook is about the American family. You want to teach that?"

Me: "Of course! Sounds like fun. Will you help me do a compare and contrast?"

And we did. Lâm Anh helped me as I learned more about the Vietnamese culture, and we often team-taught the class by comparing how the two different societies operated. Living in a foreign culture, I learned more about my own culture than I ever would have learned if I'd stayed in America. This is from the textbook:

Americans view the family as a group whose primary purpose is to advance the happiness of individual members. The result is that the needs of each individual take priority in the life of the family… What would be best for the family is not considered to be as important as what would be best for the individual… If the couple is not happy, the couple may choose to get a divorce.[9]

Oh—come on! That's not true! Americans aren't *that* shallow! I got very defensive as I read this (and some other observations) that at first blush seemed to find fault with American society.

Until…I looked…

And I realized that in America, if a spouse doesn't make me happy, get rid of him/her—and maybe find somebody else who can make me happy. Family? Kids? Naw—my happiness is more important.

The job of a spouse is to make the other spouse happy.

I'm not under the delusion that the Vietnamese society is either perfect or even better, but I also noticed that the Vietnamese view of marriage is a combination of social contract and romance. There seems to be less emphasis on "me" and more on "us." But I also know the Vietnamese marriage ideals are changing as the society becomes more Westernized.

Lâm Anh and I decided to have some fun at the beginning of one class. I started the session by saying I was the oldest son in my family. That brought nodding heads of approval.

I said my father had died many years ago, but that my mother was still alive and I loved her very much. More nodding heads of approval. "My mother is ninety years old—and she lives by herself."

An audible gasp rippled through the class. This was not good—Mr. Doug does not seem to be a very good son—he forces his mother to live alone! Especially bad because his father is dead. There is nobody to care for Mr. Doug's mother.

"My mother often says that she does not want to be a burden on her children, and she wants to live alone as long as possible."

That did it. The classroom erupted. This was almost beyond my students' ability to grasp. They lived in a collective society[10] —one that values the family, the community, and society more than the individual. They had a lot of difficulty grasping America's individualistic culture.

In America, a good child knows he must leave his parents' home when he is through with high school. Go to college, get a job, join the army—but you're not staying at home. We are raised that way from birth.

---

9 Lâm Anh compiled his text from many sources, as is normal practice in Việt Nam, where conventional textbooks are far too expensive for students. This quote came from Maryanne Keamy Datesman, JoAnn Crandall, and Edward N. Keamy, *The American Ways: An Introduction to American Culture.* (White Plains, Pearson ESL 2002).

10 Living in a collective society has nothing at all to do with living in a Communist country. Like most East Asian countries, Việt Nam's culture has been heavily influenced by Confucius, the ancient Chinese philosopher who developed a structured way for societies to govern themselves. The highest virtue in the Confucian system is filial piety—the duty to one's parents. A person subordinates himself to the greater good of the family and the village.

In Việt Nam, only the educated elite of the current generation considers leaving home to build a career. A young person is expected to stay at home until married, and even then, to stay in or around the same village. As the parents age, the eldest son has the basic responsibility to care for them, though all children should contribute. In rural areas, it is still the norm to have three or four generations living under one roof.

His name was Lộc (say *lopp*). I don't know why he was the way he was—but he was different. He was a street kid, and most street kids are extremely annoying.

"Hey—where you from?" If they can just engage the rookie tourist—the one who doesn't know better than to reply—they'll get a sale.

"You want shoe shine?" or "My sister sick" or "You gimme fie dollah"—whatever it is they are trying to get. I loved the "shoe shine" bit, as I always wore sandals while I lived in Việt Nam.

Some of these kids can be very aggressive, tugging on your clothes or stepping in front of you as you walk. There's nothing cute about these boys.

But Lộc was different—he was polite, didn't drive people crazy—and his English was very good. We had learned early on that the best thing to do if you want to help these kids is to actually feed them—don't give them money. In many cases (especially in Hồ Chí Minh City and Hà Nội), adults are handling the street kids. The adults get most of the money, and the kids stay hungry. Cindy would often buy Lộc a meal—and let him pick what he wanted from the menu. Lộc almost always chose a simple rice dish—he didn't splurge. He would eat quietly, then always say, "Thank you," when he was finished.

And Lộc seemed to have a sixth sense about where he could find us at mealtime. He didn't make a pest of himself—he didn't try to find us every day, but he knew our hangouts and where he could find us. He knew Bà Cindy was good for a meal when everything else failed.

If we were eating lunch at Phương Nam, it was not unusual to see Lộc approach us—always with a smile and a polite, "Hello." He never pestered us, but the kid was skinny, even if he was well-scrubbed and polite. Cindy would invite him to sit down with us. He could read, so he would order *cơm chiên heo* (say *come chee-in hey-oh*—fried rice with pork) or *mì xào* (say *mee sow*—fried noodles) or some other inexpensive dish. He wouldn't bolt his food, but you could tell he was hungry.

Next page: Shy smiles are what I got from this eleven-year-old girl. She and her single mother live in a one-room concrete block house built next to a putrid canal. Her mother has no husband, no land to plant vegetables, and no education—just a skill to make conical hats. The hats are not sold to tourists, because she lives too far away from them and has no motorbike to get in to Huế to sell them. Mother and daughter sell their hats in the local market—they make two hats a day, and make 20,000 Đông—a little over a dollar a day. An education will be the little girl's only way out of abject poverty. My friend Mr. Cu quietly gives Mom the tuition money—plus a little extra.

But we wondered—why did ten-year-old Lộc live on the street? We never really figured it out, but he may not actually have lived on the street, but rather was a member of a very poor family who could not afford to pay the very small tuition to put their son in school. Lộc should have started school when he was six or seven years old. The problem may have been that Lộc's parents (if he had any) couldn't afford the fee of 60,000–70,000 VND per year (approximately $4.50 to $5.00 in 2006). Worse, they wouldn't be able to buy him notebooks, pencils and a book bag—or a uniform.

A simple meal of fried rice with chicken or pork, washed down with nước chanh (lime juice) was all Lộc ever ordered.

School attendance is supposed to be mandatory, but how does a government enforce the law when parents can't afford the cost—small though it may be? After elementary school, the kids go to a secondary school, which has four grades. Besides the higher fees of $6.50 a year (plus books, pencils, uniform, etc.), entrance to a secondary school is by competitive exam.

The entire Vietnamese educational system is test-based. At the end of each year, secondary students take an exam. If they fail that one exam, they have to repeat the exam or come back the next year.

Next is high school, with three grades and an increased cost of tuition to 125,000 VND (about $8.50), and you must pass an entrance exam to enter. Some provinces require two entrance exams, while others require only one. Some of the top high schools, such as the famous Quôc Học in Huế (say *Quock Hop*), where both Hồ Chí Minh and General Giap studied, require one entrance exam. Others base their recruitment on the students' past academic records and the results of the end-of secondary school exam.

In other words, if Lộc's family was desperately poor, he stood little chance of getting the schooling he needed to break out of the poverty cycle.

But something happened for the good, though we don't know how. While on a return trip in 2008, Cindy saw Lộc on the street—wearing a school uniform. After Cindy's enthusiastic greeting, he beamed as he apologized and said, "I'm sorry. I don't have time to talk. I'm on my way to school."

Hopefully, Loc will one day be able to attend university, but if he does, the school will likely be very different from the university where we taught.

The Vietnamese educational system changed while we were there, and continues to change. Traditional learning is based on rote learning—mere memorization. Just like students at American public universities are often required to take subjects such as the "History of Texas," Vietnamese students have to take courses in "Marxist-Leninist Philosophy" and "Hồ Chí Minh Ideology," but students are merely required to memorize the material in the political courses. I could tell when the end of a semester was approaching, because I would see students off by themselves, lips moving as they tried to memorize what they thought would be on a test.

But the system is moving more toward developing critical thinking skills. As more faculty members return with advanced degrees earned in the west, the faster the change.

Western degrees are highly desirable. Many go to Australia or New Zealand for Master's degrees and doctorates. Realizing the need to have a higher education system more worthy of respect, the government recently authorized that a new "international standard" university that would guarantee academic freedom be formed in Hồ Chí Minh City. There is even the promise of recruiting *Viet kieu* (Vietnamese living overseas) academics as faculty members. That might be difficult for some older Communist Party members to accept.

Private universities were only authorized a few years ago (but cannot be owned by religious organizations), and are not considered to be up to standard. Their reputation is that they are where the lazy children of rich parents go to get a piece of paper to hang on the wall. That may change as some foreign universities have set up shop, most notably the Australian Royal Melbourne Institute of Technology. After we left in 2006, the private Phú Xuân University opened its doors in Huế, and became the first competition to the University of Huế.

Education is changing rapidly, yet it must be acknowledged that to change aspects of the system means changing the culture as well. One cannot develop critical thinkers without interaction between teacher and student—and that means students will have to ask questions, and teachers learn how to accept questions without feeling the students are disrespectful.

Like most change—it will be a challenge.

During the first semester in the spring of 2005, we lived on the Sư Phạm campus. Outside our window was one of two big classroom buildings. Solidly made of concrete, the floors of the classrooms were like those of all floors in Việt Nam—they were made of tile.

At three in the morning, you could hear people: the cleaning ladies who came in to sweep and mop and do whatever cleaning ladies do at 3:00 a.m. The talking wasn't terribly loud, but they weren't whispering either.

There were no air-conditioned classrooms. There was no glass in the windows. The doors were always open to an outside hallway. Everything was concrete and tile.

The College of Pedagogy (or Teacher's College) at the University of Huế. Admission into a Sư Phạm is difficult—only the School of Medicine requires higher entrance exam scores than the teacher's colleges. If you are smart enough to get in, you will also get the best education the country offers. Most colleges charge tuition, but a Sư Phạm education is free. Viet Nam's culture values education highly, and being a teacher is prestigious, even though the job pays poorly.

Mondays were among my favorite days on campus. The girls were required to wear an áo dài (say owe yie) to class. I very much wanted to take photos of the girls in their diaphanous dresses, but didn't want to be seen as a "dirty old man," especially being a Westerner who lived on campus. Cindy took this photo as well as most of the other photos of ladies in their áo dài.

Most girls disliked wearing the áo dài. It's not a practical garment—there are no pockets, and the long panel gets caught in bike chains and blows in the wind. As for me, I believe the áo dài is the most feminine garment ever to grace the female form.

Photo courtesy Cindy Young

Ever pull a wooden chair over a tile floor? It makes one hellacious screeching sound.

When the cleaning crew had to sweep or mop, they had to move the tables and chairs—and they did it by just pulling them across the floor.

And the screeching sound was enough to wake the dead—or at least it would awaken two Western teachers across the courtyard.

I wonder if anyone in the cleaning crew figured out what "*Lift the damned thing up*" meant.

Việt Nam is a very noisy place.

But there is a very good reason why it is noisy. The constant high humidity, combined with a lack of air conditioning, means that there is no place in the Vietnamese living room for overstuffed sofas, thick carpets and heavy drapes. Such things would soon rot.

Knowing why it is noisy doesn't help much when it is noisy. Sitting in the Mandarin Café sipping a cà phê sữa đá (say *café shoo-a da*—iced coffee with sweetened condensed milk) with Cu was enjoyable until a kid on a loud motorbike went by, ending the conversation for a few seconds, only to be delayed again when a loud diesel truck went by. The walls of the Mandarin were concrete—the floor tile—the high ceiling concrete—no drapes—no carpet—no sound-deadening ceiling tiles—and the entire front of the café opened out onto the street.

With so little difference between indoors and outdoors, the Vietnamese haven't developed an "indoor voice." In America, when the kid comes into the, house screaming at the top of her lungs, Mom says, "Use your indoor voice, Jennifer." It's one of the reasons I didn't like being in the enclosed part of the Đông Ba market—it seemed as though everybody was shouting.

Of course, in an outdoor market, the ladies are shouting—not out of anger or even to be heard above the din—but rather, because the Vietnamese are such outgoing people. In a way, they remind me of the Italians I grew up with in a Boston suburb—everybody talks at once. Until a Westerner gets used to the way Vietnamese talk, it can be unsettling. During a good conversation, if you wait until you can get a word in, you'll never have the chance to speak.

And don't expect "Please" and "Thank you" all the time, as your mother taught you. Your Vietnamese waiter may think it a bit disingenuous when you say, "Thank you," when he brings your food to the table— that's just his job. Just as foreigners may be a little put off by the bargaining that the Vietnamese love to do at market, so are the Vietnamese just a little suspicious of the constant barrage of what they consider overdone politeness.

The Perfume River floods Huế all too often. Central Việt Nam catches a lot of typhoons as they come in from the South China Sea. When the heavy tropical rains hit the nearby mountains, the river floods immediately, creating scenes like this. American homes are built of dry wall, wood and plaster, but Vietnamese homes are plain concrete, with tile floors. People merely carry their susceptible possessions upstairs, sit on their plastic chairs downstairs, and watch the world go by. When the flood waters recede, they'll spend a day or so sweeping out the mud, then moving their things back. Of course, the poorest people, especially those in the rural areas, may not live in such substantial dwellings, but generally speaking, Huế survives the floods fairly easily.

As Việt Nam's economy continues to develop, people will build nicer homes that will include items that can be ruined by floods. Such is the nature of progress.

By the fall semester in 2005, we were completely comfortable in our environment. We could get around town without a map, the xích lô drivers following us down the street trying to get us to use their services no longer bothered us, and we had a steady stream of students visiting our apartment. We had friends, a busy teaching schedule, and great students.

Culture shock? Long gone.

Both of these women are talking at the same time, and there is a third lady standing behind me as I take the picture—she, too, is part of the conversation. While it baffles me how people understand each other when they all talk at once, it works for the villagers who gather in rural markets to buy food and swap gossip.

Returning vet syndrome? Hardly ever thought about the war, except when we met the occasional veteran, through Cu, when they came through the Mandarin Café.

Problems with the heat? Only that I had strange tanning marks on my feet from wearing sandals all the time. Problems with the cold, humid winter? Bought an electric space heater.

I wrote on my blog twice a week, posting photos and stories about Việt Nam and its people. We had, by this time, mastered teaching English, were confident in our classroom skills, knew how to navigate the politics of the College of Foreign Languages, and were comfortable as mentors of our students. We were tourists no longer—we were now members of the community. We ate Vietnamese food, and though we could not speak the language, we did just fine.

In other words, life was good.

Don't They Hate Us?

Troopers of the 1st Cavalry Division jump from a "slick" (a troop-carrying helicopter) during one of the many battles against the People's Army of Viet Nam (what we called the North Vietnamese Army) in the A Shau Valley west of Huế.

I was then, and am now, proud to be a part of "The Cav," arguably the best major American unit in the war. When I joined the 1st Cav in 1969, it had left the area around Huế and was fighting in the jungle near the Cambodian border northwest of Saigon.

Photo courtesy 1st Cavalry Division. It first appeared in "The 1st Air Cavalry Division, Vietnam, August 1965 to December 1969."

The beery reunion was in full swing. Old buddies who hadn't seen each other since the war now gathered to compare white hair, paunches, photos of grandchildren—and war stories. The noise level in the hotel meeting room was high, punctuated occasionally by raucous laughter. Piles of photos from the war were scattered across tables. The wives had gone off on a shopping spree, leaving the veterans to talk openly. I sat at one table, against the wall and out of traffic. Nursing a cup of coffee rather than a beer, I talked to three other guys who had also served with Charlie Company at various times.

Bill: "Come on, Doug—I just flat don't believe you. That's BS. We damned near destroyed that country. I read somewhere that we dropped more tons of bombs on Vietnam than we dropped during all of World War II. Hell—we were caught near an Arc Light[11]—remember that? When an Arc Light hit a 'ville, there was nothing left but a huge hole in the ground."

Don: "Yeah—never understood how the gooks[12] could keep fighting after a B-52 strike. Must have been a lot of widows and sad mama-sans after one of those. I remember once when we searched a village in Bong Son for VC, and pulled little old ladies out of bunkers dug underneath their hootches. No men—just mothers, kids and old ladies. Man—they hated us! You could really see it in their eyes."

Me: "No really—the Vietnamese don't hate us today. Really!"

Bill: "Baloney. Look around this room—there are some guys who aren't at this reunion, but they were at reunions a few years ago. They died—they died of cancer from Agent Orange. Man—if we had so many guys with Agent Orange problems, the gooks must really have a problem—they're still living in it. They gotta hate us for that."

Don: "Yeah—whaddya suppose happens at My Lai every year? It's not some sort of 'Love America' festival, that's for damned sure."

Tim: "I never did anything like torch a village, but I sure saw a lot of stories about it after I got home. Man— we screwed over that country. We lost, what—fifty-eight thousand guys? How many did the NVA lose?"

---

11 GI-speak for a B-52 bomber strike. The B-52 was the largest warplane in America's arsenal, and could drop prodigious payloads. When C 2/5 Cav was caught closer than five kilometers away from an Arc Light strike in 1969, we laid on the ground in an open field while huge chunks of shrapnel lopped off the tops of nearby trees. The earth moved up and down so hard, we literally had bruises on our chests and stomachs.

12 Obviously, I do not use words like "gook" today, but most veterans use them out of habit, and do not use the words in a derogatory manner

And so the discussion went on. Despite the fact that I had lived in Việt Nam for one and a half years, none of the combat veterans believed me. I've had similar conversations with non-veterans—and even those who did not serve in the war seem to believe the Vietnamese must hate Americans.

And Việt Nam had suffered. The southern army—what we called the ARVN (Army of the Republic of Vietnam)—lost approximately a quarter of a million men. Communist forces (by government estimate) tallied over a million, one hundred thousand. By contrast, America lost over fifty-eight thousand people. The Vietnamese lost homes, businesses, sons, husbands, and brothers. No American homes were destroyed. No American businesses were bombed. Of course the Vietnamese must hate us. It's just plain common sense!

And it's like a communal guilt trip.

Americans—veterans and non-veterans alike—seem to feel that all Vietnamese must hate us. Since returning from our first trip in 2002, and after speaking to many of these veterans and hearing so many of them ask, *"Don't they hate us?"* I now expect the subject to come up in conversation.

When I am asked that question now, my reply is another question: "Why would they hate us?"

And I find most veterans have never really thought about it—it's an assumption that the Vietnamese must hate us. Maybe it links back to our remembrances—our remembrances frozen in time—as well as not knowing anything about the country after America's departure. Our memories are filled with scenes of poverty, misery, burned villages, and destitute peasants. It's natural to assume the people still live in poverty, and that we caused their misery. America turned off its lens after our troops left in 1973, and only glanced briefly at Vietnam again in 1975, when the south fell. After that, our reference to the country was in relation to the war, especially before and after each subsequent war, when pundits talked about the "lessons of Vietnam." After Grenada, Somalia, Panama, and the Gulf War, as well as wars in Iraq and Afghanistan, news outlets trumpeted only reminders that America lost a war in Vietnam, but never told us what was going on inside the country. Even when America and Việt Nam re-established diplomatic relations in 1995—and even though our first ambassador was Pete Peterson, a former POW of the North Vietnamese who spent six years of confinement and torture in the infamous Hanoi Hilton—any stories about the country named Việt Nam were buried on Page eight of Section C of the daily newspaper.

Do the Vietnamese hate us? Quite the contrary—the Vietnamese love America and Americans. With only 6 percent of its population over the age of sixty-five, a median age of twenty-seven, and approximately 75 percent of the population of eighty-eight million having been born since 1975, the vast majority of Vietnamese have no recollection of the war.

But we Americans also put our own spin on events, because we know so little about the country. To Americans, the war is important, but to older Vietnamese, the linchpin of their time is not the war—the central memory is 1975, when the old southern government fell and the country was reunited. Whether northern victor or southern loser, it is 1975 and the next ten years that stand out in their memories. It is that decade of despair that they remember with acrimony.

Bitter southerners lost everything, but they didn't lose everything to the Americans—they lost what they had to a carpetbagger government from the north. Many southerners fled the country, becoming the boat people—the Vietnamese diaspora that sent them to Australia, France, Canada, and America. For those who stayed, the country sank deeper into financial ruin as the successors to Hồ Chí Minh tried to make socialism work. Việt Nam became embroiled in its own "Vietnam" in a protracted war in Cambodia, sapping resources made even thinner by the loss of China as a patron country. The Vietnamese invasion of Cambodia so incensed the Chinese that they sought to punish Việt Nam. During February and March, 1979, the Chinese army invaded Việt Nam—and suffered 6,954 killed and 14,800 wounded, as the battle-hardened Vietnamese army repelled them.

America—I have news for you. We were not the last enemy to fight against the Vietnamese—they fought their last war against their ancient foe, the Chinese. Did America cause Vietnam's agony? Of course we were part of it, but we caused it no more than Cambodia, China, and Vietnam's own leadership.

I often spent Saturday mornings with Dr. Chương, the former chair of the History department at the College of Education. During one of our conversations about current affairs, he said to look for Việt Nam to openly ask the United States to put troops into Cam Ranh Bay if China invaded Taiwan. I damned near fell out of my chair when he said that. I was then told of the deep suspicions the Vietnamese have toward China, and I reminded myself that Việt Nam's last war was against China.

There are no American troops in Cam Ranh Bay, but there has been a lot of military cooperation. The guided missile destroyer, USS Lassen, docked at Đa Nẵng in 2009. There was some irony in this event—the captain of the Lassen was Commander H. B. Le—a Vietnamese born in Huế, who escaped in 1975, when his family fled the oncoming Communists. Le's father had been a senior officer in the old southern navy. The ship is named after Clyde Lassen, a naval aviator awarded the Medal of Honor for his actions during the Vietnam War. In 2010, another destroyer visited—this one named the USS John McCain.[13]

During my 2003 visit back to Việt Nam, I was chatting with an official of the University of Đa Nẵng, with whom I had been working for a month. During the previous three weeks, I had been treated to wonderful hospitality by the university. As I prepared to leave, I told him how amazed I was to be treated in such a manner—especially since I was an American. He snorted, made a wry face, and then said, "You Americans think you are the center of the universe. We fought the Chinese occupiers for nine hundred years, fought the French for one hundred years—and the Americans were here for only twelve years. You are only a blip on our radar screen."

Nhi (say *Nyee*) was a fourth-year student working on her senior year research paper. Cindy helped her with the research—Nhi was at our apartment often. As a way of thanking Cindy for the help, she invited us to lunch at her parents' home—an invitation we accepted with pleasure. Nhi's translation skills were put to the test, because her family spoke no English and our Vietnamese was nonexistent. As expected, the meal was fresh and delicious, and as is the way of the Huế people, there was far too much food.

---

13 The ship is not named for Senator McCain, the naval aviator who spent six years in a North Vietnamese prison after being shot down. His name is John McCain III. The ship is named after his father and grandfather, both navy admirals.

But conversation was stilted. We had little in common except for Nhi, and I had to think of something to say. Noticing a framed certificate on the wall, and knowing her father was retired from the city government, I asked Nhi if it was given as a remembrance of his service.

After an awkward silence that made me very uncomfortable, she said quietly, "It thanks my father for his service as a revolutionary fighter."

I was having lunch with a Vietcong!

Nhi, like all our students, was aware I had been a soldier and had fought in the war. The students could not have cared less. The war had happened long before they were born, and all they knew about it was what they learned in school. But this situation was different—and Nhi was cautious as she told her father what I had asked about the certificate. She went on to tell him I had been an American soldier.

I knew the exact instant he understood. A huge smile erupted on his face. It was obvious that he was excited to be talking with a former American soldier. Nhi struggled to keep up with the questions and answers. We both wanted to know where the other had fought—we really wanted to know if we had fought against each other.

"When were you in Vietnam?" (He wanted to know if I had been in Vietnam after he became a Vietcong.)

"Did you ever fight against Americans who always flew in helicopters and wore big patches on their sleeves?" (I wanted to find out if he had fought against the 1st Cav, which had operated in the Huế area.)

"Did your Vietcong unit ever come south to Tay Ninh?" (More specifically, I was curious to know if we had fought against each other.)

"Were you wounded?" (We both had been.)

The lunch went on much longer than planned—fueled by a few beers.[14] He brought out a photo of himself, and I couldn't help but think of American young men and what they did on the night before they went into military service. Nhi's father was not conscripted by the Vietcong—he volunteered, just as many American men did. He was a member of a regional unit that fought in and around Thừa Thiên (say *Too-ah Tee-an*) Province. Better equipped and trained than the poorly armed local VC who stayed in their villages, the regional forces were mid-level units that stayed in a four- or five-province area, but did not move to other parts of the south to fight against the Americans and the southern army.

Hugs and beer-drinking may strike some people as odd behavior for two old men who once tried to kill each other. (That wasn't actually true—I was never near Huế during the war, but if I had been and my unit had faced his, there is no doubt we would have tried to kill each other.)

---

14 Only Nhi's father Nguyễn Đoàn, drank beer. During the one and a half years we lived in in Việt Nam in 2005–06, I did not drink alcohol. It was a policy of the teaching agency we worked with—and a good policy. Việt Nam has a real problem with its cultural tolerance of drunken men. Our agency wished to maintain its reputation of respectability and responsibility toward the youth of the universities. In 2003, while working with the University of Đa Nẵng, I had had a bit of beer during lunch on more than one occasion, making for some uncomfortable situations.

Like other young men before they enter military service, Nhi's father spent his last free night with buddies, all of whom were joining the Liberation Army. They did what all young men do—they drank lots of beer, chased girls, and had fun. The next morning, they said their goodbyes to families, and then walked into the jungle west of Huế to begin their training.

I wonder if one of their mothers asked them to have the photo taken in case one or all of them didn't come home.

Photo courtesy Nguyễn Đoàn

But nobody understands a soldier like another soldier. We both understood, without speaking, that the other had been dirty, hungry, terrified—had hated Americans/Vietcong—had missed their families very much—had thought our superiors were idiots on occasion—and had suffered from our experiences. It was a fraternity we belonged to—a club to which we had paid dues in our youth. No amount of money could now pay those dues. Nobody but soldiers from that war can be members of our club. Nguyễn Đoàn does not hate his former enemy—and I most certainly do not hate him. We were brothers from different countries. The war was over—and it was not the last time I was to have that thought.

Remembrances of war are generational. The old people of Việt Nam today doubt the kids could do what they did, or endure the suffering.

I was reminded again of how little Vietnamese young people care about the war when I visited a military museum in Quảng Trị City, the site of one of the most vicious battles of the war in 1972—a battle that cost thousands of civilian lives. (American troops were not involved—it took place after most of our combat units had been withdrawn. Only a few advisors were on the ground, but B-52 bombers provided air support.) South Vietnamese forces and American bombers expended the equivalent of six Hiroshima bombs before defeating the northerners in that campaign. The old Quảng Trị citadel took most of the punishment, and is today the site of both the museum and a peace memorial.

All those bombs and all that destruction must mean all Vietnamese hate us, right?

As I wandered around the displays in the museum, camera in hand, one of the young people I was with approached me with a big grin on her face. She asked me to follow her to a static display of mannequins dressed in uniforms, most of them striking heroic poses. Pointing at my camera, and with a big grin on her face—the young lady posed for a photograph.

If something similar had happened at The Wall in Washington, my fellow veterans would have been horrified—and no doubt said some strong words to the offending youngster about her lack of respect. There were no Vietnamese veterans in the museum at that moment, but if there had been, I imagine their reaction would have been similar to that of their American counterparts at The Wall. They would have been very angry.

If Americans wonder whether the Vietnamese hate us, I sometimes wonder why the Vietnamese don't hate the French, who inflicted far greater damage on the country than the United States did. The French sapped the resources from Việt Nam, introduced opium to the population (and built a refinery to produce it), created a whole class of indentured servants by taking people from their farms to work the rubber plantations, and tried to ensure future control of the country by denying education to all but a few elite.

Then came Điện Biên Phủ, (say *Dee-in Bee-in Foo*) a small city in the extreme northwest corner of the country. In 1954, it was merely a valley where a few members of indigenous tribes lived, but the Việt Minh (short for "League for the Independence of Vietnam") lured the French into a major battle there. France's ignoble defeat ended French rule.

By chance, I was at the battleground on May 7, the fifty-second anniversary of the French surrender. Unlike Quảng Trị, where I did not see a Vietnamese veteran, I saw one at Điện Biên Phủ. He was an old man—older than me, and from a war previous to mine. As I watched, his sons and grandsons carefully lifted him atop an old French tank.

He sat alone, pondering what had happened when he was a young man fighting for the independence of his people from France. Maybe he was pondering old friends he lost—maybe some of his buddies were in the nearby cemetery. There are six hundred and forty Viet Minh grave markers in that cemetery, but only four of those have names on the markers.[15]

Old soldiers do that: wonder about the friends who never had the chance to grow old, be grandfathers, and get grey hair. We wonder why we lived and they died—*if that bullet had been three inches in another direction, it would have been me and not him*. Such are the thoughts I imagined going through his mind.

I understood—but I doubt any of the American young people I was with at Điện Biên Phủ could even guess at our thoughts.

There is a remarkable plot of land at Điện Biên Phủ—remarkable as a possible harbinger of things to come for America. It is a memorial erected to the members of the French Foreign Legion who died in battle in the First Indochina War of 1946–1954. Built by an association of Foreign Legion veterans, today the plot is tended by the Vietnamese.

---

15 There are many of these military cemeteries throughout the country, well-tended, and with incense burned before the grave markers. To the great discredit of the victorious Communists, the cemeteries of the southerners have been bulldozed under—only the victors are honored. This is doubly outrageous in a culture that must honor its ancestors.

The Vietnamese consider themselves to be a Francophone country. They harbor no resentment toward the French, just as they harbor none toward America. Large numbers of French tourists visit Việt Nam every year.

Such is the forgiving nature of the Vietnamese. They do not hate the French—they have moved on.

And I wonder—could there ever be a memorial to our American dead on Vietnamese soil? It would seem the Vietnamese might be amenable—would Americans be willing?

Such forgiveness has its limits—there are some Vietnamese who do not especially love America—but the lack of forgiveness may come from unexpected places.

My friend Cu and I had taken an entire day to roam the countryside to take photos. As we rode our motorbikes south along the sandy barrier island on the South China Sea, we came across an old pagoda. Cu wanted some photos of the gate, which bore some sort of ancient inscription that mattered little to me. As I waited for him to chat with the monks and take his pictures, I saw a man about my age sitting in a wheel chair. He was quietly watching me from the far side of the courtyard.

"Cu, why is that man staring at me?"

"Probably because he doesn't see Westerners out here in the countryside very often."

And I asked Cu to politely ask the man how he had lost his legs. The man had been a *thiêu úy* (say *tee yeu whee*) in the old southern army—a second lieutenant—a fellow infantry officer. He'd lost his legs to an anti-personnel mine in 1974.

With no family any more, the wounded veteran was cared for by the monks, and certainly got no help from the Communist government. We chatted through Cu for a while, and I told him I, too, had been an infantry officer during the war. I was to discover that despite being a double amputee, he had been imprisoned for three years in a Communist "re-education camp" after the war. After a few

Photo courtesy Phan Cu

moments, he looked at me, said something quietly to Cu, and then waited for the translation. Cu paused, seemed uncomfortable, and then spoke—

"He wants to know where the Americans are now."

Stunned and embarrassed by how my country had deserted him, I slowly came to my feet. Though I was unable to think of anything to say, I'm sure my face said everything.

For a soldier, the salute is an expression of respect. I stood in front of the man who had once been a comrade-in-arms, came to a position of attention, raised my hand in salute, and held it until he returned it. I left with tears in my eyes.

Don't they hate us?

I had visited the old battlefield at Khe Sanh—been to the Vietcong tunnels of Cu Chi—strolled through the war museum at Quảng Trị—toured the old French battlefield at Điện Biên Phủ—revisited the mountain we soldiers had called Nui Ba Den in 1969—sought the scene of my old unit's biggest combat losses at Bong Son—taken a taxi to my 1967 stompin' grounds near Bình Chánh—even visited the infamous Hanoi Hilton where so many American prisoners had been held.

For a guy who said he didn't think much about the war, I sure visited a lot of wartime places. Why did I travel to find them?

As I've said, I have a poor memory, and remember few names or dates, yet obviously, one does not go through combat without some memories. After all, I am a veteran—the war was my first connection to the country, and I wanted to see how things look today. I'd never had expectations of finding anything of the war, and had no emotional needs to satisfy. I was just curious. Of course, being an amateur historian proved another draw to those old battlefields.

One would think that merely standing next to the six-lane highway leading into today's Bình Chánh District would conjure memories—but there is no resemblance between the industrial area today and the small rice-growing village where I spent nine months in 1967.

Sergeant Ben White, Specialist Bill Paquette, and a Ranger from the old southern army on patrol near Binh Chanh in April, 1967. They were walking on the dikes between dry rice fields. From ancient times until today, the fields are flooded during the rainy season.

Photo courtesy Bill Paquette

But back then, I was in a war. Soldiers I knew well and cared about were being killed and wounded. Sergeant Ben White had been one of my squad leaders in 1967. One evening, after the nightly operations orders had been given to the sergeants, Ben came up to me—

"Hey LT (Say *El Tee*),[16] I just want to say I really enjoyed working with you."

---

16 "LT" was the short slang for "lieutenant." Ben was not being disrespectful to me—the term was often used among the tightly knit combat units I served with. Ben was killed on July 10, 1967. He was a year older than me.

"What the hell you talking about, Ben?"

"Just wanted to say goodbye. We're gonna get hit tonight, and I'll buy the farm."

"Damn, Ben! Don't talk like that! That's crazy, man!"

"It's okay, LT—it really is. It's cool."

Sure enough, as the ambush patrol was on the way out, they themselves were ambushed. Ben was killed immediately. Bill Paquette had been my radio operator up until he was promoted to sergeant a few days prior, and he was going out to learn how to run a patrol from Ben. Bill humped the radio—and though badly wounded, he was saved by the radio on his back that absorbed most of the shrapnel from the opening blast. He endured having a VC kill team search him, thinking him dead. His salvation was that two Vietcong argued over the two packs of cigarettes they found in his pockets.

That first tour in 1967 was quite different from what I was to endure in 1969. On my first tour, we had constant daily contact with non-combatant Vietnamese people. During my second tour, we had no contact with ordinary civilians—if we saw a Vietnamese, we shot him. There were no villages, just jungle. Our enemy was no longer a local farmer who was a VC by night, but rather a well-trained and well-equipped soldier from the north. No more pernicious booby traps—in 1969, it was straight combat against rockets, rocket-propelled grenades, mortars, and lots of large-caliber machine guns. Though the battles of 1967 and 1969 were both deadly, they were very different wars.

After spending thirteen months at Fort Campbell, Kentucky, in between my two tours in Vietnam, I took command of Charlie Company in April, 1969. My first mission assignment was to helicopter into an empty field where we built LZ (Landing Zone) Ike, a mini-fortress of sandbag bunkers encircling six artillery guns and our battalion headquarters. Ike was to prove a thorn in the side of the enemy—it was located near the Mustang Trail, a network of trails hidden from aerial view by the thick jungle canopy. Legions of North Vietnamese ferried supplies of weapons, food, ammunition, and all the other necessities of war to hidden supply caches. From them, their comrades could gird themselves for attacks on Saigon, Bien Hoa, and the other cities and bases in the south. Our job was to find these caches, destroy them, and thereby cut off the enemy's logistical nose.

Our enemy did not stand by quietly while we searched for and found their supplies. They fought us ferociously and frequently. They sniped at us, threw mass attacks against LZ Ike, and rocketed our big base at Tay Ninh. Our normal mode was to spend fifteen days in the field trying to find the NVA, then rotate back to LZ Ike for five days, replacing another company as the protection force for the jungle outpost. Out in the field, we would make another helicopter assault into a new area every three days, and we would get fresh supplies of food, water, ammunition—and new personnel. It was a system designed to keep constant pressure on the North Vietnamese.

And it worked—worked very well indeed. We were in regular firefights. Carrying 125 pounds of food, water, and ammunition on our backs, hacking through the thick jungle, wearing uniforms that would literally rot off our backs after ten to fifteen days of soaking up our sweat, digging a new foxhole every night, and staying awake for all but a few hours at night, the troopers of Charlie Company were a sample of young America.

DON'T THEY HATE US?

Most didn't want to be there, but while in the army, they did their job and did it well. When engaged in combat, they fought heroically and they fought hard. The American GI is a tough, smart, and relentless enemy.

When our sister unit, B Company, was hit hard on June 19, we were sent to help them out. The jungle was very thick—there were no places near B Company where we could land helicopters. We had to hump overland to get to our beleaguered buddies. By the next morning, they were still in contact, had a number of dead and wounded, and were running low on ammunition. Two helicopters were sent out with extra ammunition for us to deliver to them, but when the birds tried to land near us, enemy snipers opened fire on them. We called in helicopter gunships to suppress the fire, off loaded the supply choppers, split the extra load of ammo amongst ourselves, and kept on moving toward the embattled B Company.

It's tricky trying to join up with a friendly unit while under fire. The troopers of B Company knew we were near, but with the very limited visibility, caused by the thick jungle, we needed a way to identify ourselves. The last thing any of us wanted was for two American units to start shooting at each other. I called B Company's commander on the radio

Comanche: "Ridge Runner 6, this is Comanche 6—over."

Ridge Runner 6: "Runner 6—go ahead, Comanche."

Comanche: "I just fired some willie peter[17] air burst rounds to locate myself. You see them?"

Ridge Runner 6: "Affirmative."

Using his compass, Ridge Runner 6 spotted the two air bursts that had been fired to known locations, triangulated his position, and found it on his map. I did the same thing, and then we used a code book to encrypt our messages and share our locations. We figured we were close to each other. He also told me he was not receiving enemy fire from the direction we were approaching. That meant that most likely, there were no enemy troops between us. After setting up some simple passwords the troopers could use to identify each other, we warily—but safely—joined up with them.

As our men gave food and ammo to the guys in the other company, we two commanders hastily split up our part of the circle defense for the night, letting our soldiers have what little daylight remained to dig in before night fell.

And it didn't take long to realize it would be a very long night. Normally, the North Vietnamese would spend a while planning attacks, but this night, they began probing our positions right after sunset. The enemy wanted us to shoot back so they could locate our foxholes by the muzzle flashes of our rifles. During some of those mini-firefights, First Sergeant "Red" Allen would taunt the North Vietnamese, and shoot back at them with his Chinese-made AK-47 rifle. But the NVA had been fighting B Company for two days—they knew where Ridge Runner was located, and they knew we had joined them.

---

17 GI speak for the letters W and P, which meant white phosphorous. White phosphorous artillery shells do not kill by showering the enemy with shrapnel—they kill by burning the flesh. WP shells explode in a white cloud. By setting them to explode in the air, we make the white cloud easy to see. Military purists will know that the phonetic word for the letter W is Whiskey, not Willie. But then again, many of us were not purists – we were typical Americans who stretched things a bit.

A mortar is a type of small artillery piece. It launches explosive rounds high into the sky, creating a long wait between the time one hears the hollow "thoonk" sound of the mortar being fired and the explosion when it lands. We heard that first "thoonk," and dived for our foxholes. When the mortar attack came, it was very heavy. The 3rd Platoon caught the brunt of it. One mortar round landed right in the platoon's command post foxhole. The NVA also fired B-40 rocket-propelled grenades into the perimeter. After the mortars and B-40 firing ceased, the NVA kept up the pressure with small fights around the perimeter, but there was no ground assault, probably because we had lots of artillery fire and helicopters raining steel death on top of them.

Three fine men lost their lives in that attack. Sergeant Dennis Resinger was a Squad Leader with 3rd Platoon. Lieutenant Kenneth Susmarski was not technically a member of Comanche—he was undergoing "on-the-job training" before being given his permanent assignment. He had been in Vietnam only fifteen days. Private Allyn Stevens wasn't a member of Comanche either. He was normally a medic with Ridge Runner, but was sent out to us on a temporary basis when one of our regular medics went to Tay Ninh for new eyeglasses. When our regular medic came back, he was sent to B Company so he could then join up with us again. As fate would have it, with both C and B companies in the same perimeter, the two decided to move back to their respective units the next morning. The decision cost Allyn his life.

Both the Platoon Leader, Lieutenant Paul, and the Platoon Sergeant, Staff Sergeant Richard Fujiwara, were severely wounded. The LT was brought to my command post with a sucking chest wound. The only way he could breathe was if we propped him up and put pieces of plastic over the holes in his chest and back. He wanted a cigarette, but some strong words from me and from the Senior Medic, Jerry "Doc" Watson, helped change his mind. LT Paul would have died that night, if not for the bravery of a Medevac crew. Though there was no place to set down a helicopter, a small landing zone was blown with C4 plastic explosive wrapped around the right trees. Even with some sniper fire coming in, and the tips of the blade slapping surrounding tree limbs, the bird came in, picked Paul up, and got him to a hospital.

During the attack, many of the shells burst in the tree branches overhead, showering us with shrapnel. Even if you were down in your foxhole, you could get hit. It was one of those tree bursts that planted some shrapnel in my back, just below my right shoulder blade.

"Doc" Watson tended the more seriously wounded before he patched me up. I had more than enough to do to keep my mind off the pain—the shooting was still going on, though it tapered off to mere sniper fire after a while. Jerry was the senior medic with the company, and well-known for his incredible bravery under fire.

Doc: "Damn, Six, you're not hurt bad, but you're also lucky the shrapnel didn't penetrate much further, or it would have hit your lungs."

Me: "Doc—don't even think about sending me in on the Medevac bird! I'm not going!"

Doc: "Send you in? Hell no—all I wanna do is pull it out, saturate the wound with disinfectant, give you a stitch or two, then kiss you on the forehead and tell you to get your lazy ass back to work. Naw—you aren't going on sick call cuz of me!"[18]

---

[18] I am not a hero—being wounded does not make me a hero—but Jerry "Doc" Watson is a hero to me. I regularly saw Doc expose himself to enemy fire for the sake of the wounded troopers he cared for. But Doc himself was wounded and is still wounded today. Suffering from a serious case of Post-Traumatic Stress Disorder, Jerry is now an inmate in a Washington State prison. He sought some relief by writing a book, but "Six Band-Aid" has yet to find a publisher. A gifted artist, Jerry is currently painting his impression of the little girl seen weaving a conical hat seen on Page 92. I'm no hero—but Doc Watson was then, is now, and will always be my hero.

Doc stitched me up while keeping an eye on LT Paul and the other seriously wounded men who had been brought to the command post as a collection point for the Medevac bird. A few days later, we were sent back to LZ Ike. My wound was a little sore by then. When the battalion surgeon (a physician) looked at it, he raised hell because an infection had started. Of course, Doc had done exactly the right thing in letting me stay in the field—I needed to be with my men. I had a strong bond with the men of Comanche—and still do today. The infection healed, and I went back to work.

Like any vet, I have stories—lots of them. I am not a robot who has conveniently forgotten the hard times and grim events. It would be disingenuous on my part to say that I've never had any memories of my wartime experiences. It would be equally disingenuous to say that the main reason I returned to live and teach in Việt Nam was to be near those memories. But there is little doubt such memories played a part in my desire to see other battlefields.

And when I saw those battlefields, I realized again that the war is over.

It is over for Americans, and for the Vietnamese.

And they don't hate us, despite our blood-soaked history.

I found out more about how the Vietnamese react to the war through one of the other Americans living in Huế. James Sullivan is much too young to be a veteran of the war. Jim met his bride Thuy (say *Twee*) in 1992, when he and a buddy pedaled their bikes from Hồ Chí Minh City to Hà Nội with the intention of writing a story for a cycling magazine. When they came through Huế, boy met girl, and romance took its course.

Thuy's father had been an artillery sergeant in the southern army. In 1972, he was badly wounded and left for dead when his unit was overrun in Quảng Trị. Mr. Bang survived to see his daughter become involved with an American man. When it became obvious that the relationship had grown serious, he talked to his daughter.

His comment to Thuy? "Americans are very good at leaving."[19]

My personal recollections are not always well met by other veterans. It is my belief that the Vietnamese have long gotten over the war—even those who are of age to remember it. Some veterans find that hard to believe. One of them, a man who harbors deep suspicions of the "mainstream media," told me he had watched an ABC News television special about Senator John McCain, in which a former guard at McCain's Hanoi prison had said he hated McCain and wished him dead. My only rejoinder to my fellow veteran is that he could either believe the "main stream media," or he could believe someone who actually lived in Việt Nam. I have no doubt there are some, especially in the north, who harbor hatred for America; I can only say that in my one and a half years of living in Việt Nam, and during the many subsequent trips, I have never once been aware of anything negative being said to or about me. Nor have I talked to any other returning Vietnam vet who encountered resentment.

While at a bank in Huế one day, exchanging some money, I watched a television commercial advertising a special program to be shown, about the end of the American War and the fall of Saigon. Ironically, the video clip I saw was taken from an American helicopter. But the Liberation Day festivities are no more anti-American when the Vietnamese show pictures of American troops than our Fourth of July celebrations are anti-British when pictures of Red Coats are shown.

---

19 James tells this story in his book, "Over the Moat: Love Among the Ruins of Imperial Vietnam," Picador 2004 on Page 67.

"Humpin' the weeds" as the commanding officer of Company C, 2nd Battalion, 5th Cavalry Regiment, 1st Cavalry Division. Break time shows me closest to the camera, with my two radio operators next to me, and the artillery radioman nearby.

Photo courtesy Doug Hendrixson

What Americans remember as the fall of Saigon on April 30, 1975, the Vietnamese call Liberation Day. Because the next day is May first—the International Workers' day celebrated by Communists around the world—it makes for a nice, long four-day weekend. There are certainly ceremonies marking the event, and old veterans (only former liberation soldiers—southern veterans are still held in official contempt) can sometimes be seen wearing their medals, but for most people, it's a time to travel, go to the beach, or just hang out.

Think Fourth of July in America.

On our first Liberation Day in Việt Nam in 2005, the day could not be ignored. While it is not something we dwelt on or even thought about frequently, the fact remained that we two old soldiers were in Việt Nam on April 30th—the thirtieth anniversary of the fall of Saigon. That day marked the end of the war, the end of the old Republic of Vietnam, and the beginning of today's Socialist Republic of Việt Nam.

We watched the elaborate celebrations in Huế, feeling a sense of loss for those young Americans who left their blood on Vietnamese soil. We knew some Vietnamese in the south did not share in the joy of reunification. Yet we were also seeing a country bursting at the seams with energy and change. We watched young people moving forward at a breakneck pace that would astound most Americans.

I remain proud of my service. I consider it a badge of honor to be called a Vietnam vet, and I never hid my past from my students.

I was also proud to be in Việt Nam, working with the people to move their country ahead.

I tried to be a good soldier. I tried to be a good teacher. Việt Nam is woven into the fabric of my life.

On that first Liberation Day in Huế, I realized again that the war was really over. It was not the last time I was to have that thought. I have moved on from the war—and pray my fellow veterans can do that too.

117

And it really was a long time ago.

Just like the old GI forks and the boats made from the aluminum external fuel tanks of American jets, there are a few other reminders of the war that are still out in the open.

Quảng Trị Province was the northernmost part of the old South Vietnam—think the DMZ and Khe Sanh. Today it is one of the poorest provinces in the country, and one of the few places where there are still reminders of the war. Signs warn farmers and children about unexploded ordnance, but people are still being injured—and killed—by bombs, grenades and artillery shells left many years ago. The towns and cities are safe, but the countryside is not. A tourist in an air-conditioned bus on her way to see the old Khe Sanh Combat Base will not see these signs—one must be away from the main roads. There are de-mining teams at work today. There was a German group we saw regularly in Huế, plus there is another funded by the Vietnam Veterans of America.

Strangely, I never saw nor heard of a team from China helping to find the old ordnance. Their hand grenades were infamous for having a lot of duds. China supplied most of the small arms to the Communist forces, but there doesn't seem to be any pressure on them to help clean up the mess.

Today, I live in deep south Texas, near the city of Edinburg. A street, an elementary school, and a park are named after Freddy Gonzalez—Marine Sergeant Alfredo Gonzalez. Sergeant Gonzalez was posthumously awarded the Medal of Honor for a series of heroic acts in February, 1968, during the initial stages of the Tet Offensive—in Huế. He died in a French school across the street from a Catholic church. Both the school building and the church are still standing. The church has been completely rebuilt—the school repaired too, but not as spiffily as the church—and the grade school is now run by the government. The dull red buildings indicate they were built in the French era—the yellow buildings were built much more recently.

And there is another legacy of the war—a legacy that has affected many American veterans, a legacy that provides still another reason for the Vietnamese to hate us: the legacy of Agent Orange. While law suits have been settled in America, the Vietnamese wonder why they cannot sue—and win—damages from American chemical companies.

Trâm (say *Drum*) was another of my wonderful students. She took on the task of working with a school that trained handicapped people so they could support themselves. Many of those in the school were second generation victims of Agent Orange, born with physical and mental shortcomings.

The black and white photo was taken by an American Marine at the end of the fighting in Huế. The photo was given to me by Cu, who got it from a visiting veteran. The Tet Offensive of 1968—an event credited with turning the tide of American public opinion against the war—was bloodiest in Huế. Communist forces held parts of the city for a month, and were only dislodged after brutal close quarters fighting.

Trần Hưng Đạo Street was then and is now a main thoroughfare. The divided four-lane road is bordered by the big Đông Ba market on one side and numerous prosperous shops on the other.

Forty-two years have passed between the taking of the picture at the top in 1968, and 2010, when the picture at the bottom was taken. My son was eight months old during the Tet Offensive. Today he is a new grandfather.

Núi Bà Đen (say Noo-ee Bah Den), the Black Virgin Mountain, arises by itself from the plains in Tay Ninh Province northwest of Saigon near the Cambodian border. Seen here from the large Tay Ninh base camp, it was the seminal landmark for American soldiers. American forces had a radio relay station on top, and we controlled the base, but Communist forces controlled the middle band around the mountain.

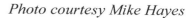

Photo courtesy Mike Hayes

Today, a gondola takes vacationing Vietnamese to the top of the mountain. The bucolic surroundings are quiet. The mountain has special significance to the Vietnamese. Legend has it that around 1900, during the time of the French, a beautiful young peasant girl fell in love with a fine young man. However, the local land owner, put in power by the French, wanted to add her to his collection of wives. Rather than submit, the girl ran away to the mountain. When found by the landowner's henchmen, she jumped to her death. Nobody knows her name—she was just the "Lady in Black," "Bà" meaning "woman," and "den" meaning "black."

This photo of the bridges at Bong Son was taken in 1968. The uppermost structure was a railroad bridge, and the other a road bridge for National Route One. Both were kept under close guard by American soldiers because they were part of the main north-south road and the rail links within South Vietnam.

Photo courtesy Don Jensen

I was standing on another bridge in 2003 when I took this picture of the old road bridge. Since then, the bridge I was standing on to take the photo has been replaced.

Though I was never there during the war, because I joined later, Company C 2/5 Cavalry was there in 1967, and suffered many casualties. Today, Bồng Sơn is still a small town.

Not all instances of mental retardation or body deformities were caused by Agent Orange—I challenge some of the assumptions of the Vietnamese government that they are—but it is also obvious that considerable damage has been and continues to be done by the chemical used to defoliate the jungle.

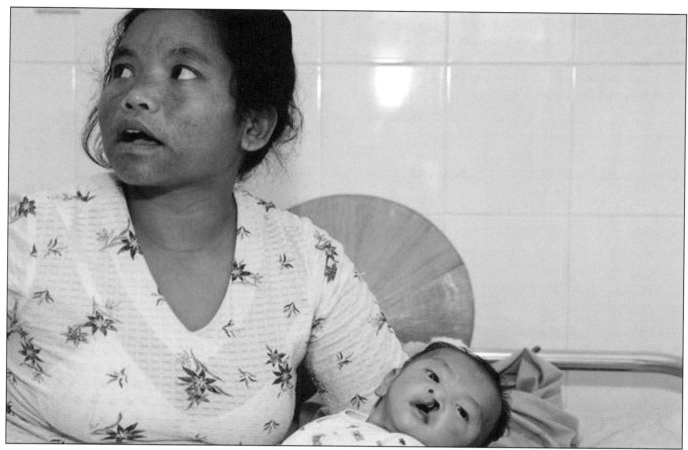

This is the third child with severe deformities delivered to this mother. She is a member of a mountain tribe—what American soldiers called Montagnards—from the A Shau valley. The scene of frequent and heavy fighting, the A Shau (say aw shau) was liberally sprayed with Agent Orange. Whether the birth defects are the legacy of dioxin, of her malnutrition caused by her eating only cassava root during her pregnancy, or of inbreeding within the small village where she functioned as the local prostitute, may never be known. The baby died three days after this photo was taken, from a congenital heart defect.

Interestingly, the school where Trâm volunteers her time is operated solely by the Vietnamese. Except for donations from a few Americans, the school is funded and operated by caring members of the new Vietnamese middle class.

As she proudly showed me through the buildings, I asked Trâm if she knew what caused the problems with the school's students. Trâm smiled, and said it was from the American War. A bigger smile, then she said, "Yes, I know you were a soldier here, Mr. Doug."

Don't they hate us?

After our first trip in 2002, I took another trip in March, 2003, to work on a project with the University of Đa Nẵng.

And I was there when the U. S. invaded Iraq.

The Bamboo Green Hotel—just down the street from Christy's Cool Spot, the Australian-owned bar and restaurant that advertised its air conditioning to attract the Western expatriates who lived in Đa Nẵng. After work each day at the university, I'd wander down the street, get myself a couple of bottles of Tiger Beer, then go back and flop down on the bed, turn on the tube, and check CNN for the latest news on the run-up to a war getting started in Iraq.

New to television was the "embedded journalist," and CNN had one of theirs with a spearhead unit—the 3rd Battalion of the 7th Infantry Regiment. It was an infantry unit mounted in armored personnel carriers racing across the deserts of Iraq toward Baghdad.

Or, as we used to call it in 1966–67, "the 3rd of the 7th."

My old unit was part of the beginning of a new war—and CNN had live coverage of the 3/7 Infantry making a dash across the Iraqi desert, firing on the occasional Iraqi army unit while heading for Baghdad. My old unit was shooting in a new war, while I sat in my hotel room in the country where I had been once in a war with that same unit.

Weird!

Early in my trip to Đa Nẵng, I had been the guest of the retired president of the University of Đa Nẵng and the current Director of the Department for Continuing Education—the same Mr. Dung (say *Yoom*) who had said America is just a blip on the Vietnamese radar. These gentlemen treated me to lunch at one of the nicest restaurants in Đa Nẵng—a beautiful place with great service and better food. During the meal, the staff began to wheel out large television sets on carts. On cue, the TVs were turned on to a Vietnamese news channel. I couldn't understand the language, but I knew what the video was. While I sat in a Vietnamese restaurant, surrounded by Vietnamese people, I watched a new American war begin.

I was the only American in the room.

Nobody shot me disapproving glances.

Don't they hate us?

No—they don't. The nation is full of young people who have no time to hate—they only have time to get a good education, find a decent paying job that will allow them to buy the hippest clothes, a new smart phone, a better motorbike—and eventually get married and buy a car.

Even the old folks don't hate us.

Tân (say *Dunn*) was born in 1946. He never had the chance to finish high school—the war took him away from such normal pursuits. When the southern army drafted him, he had a choice—go into the army, or work for an American Rural Development Team.

He didn't want to be cannon fodder—he didn't pick the army. He worked directly for the Americans, part of a small team that traveled around Thừa Thiên Province helping farmers grow better crops. His boss was a U.S. Marines Corps officer. For this, he spent three years in a Communist re-education camp, and upon his release, found his wife had thought him dead and had remarried.

His country had lost the war.

He went to prison for helping the enemy.

He incurred physical injury to his back and legs from prison beatings.

He lost his family.

He lost his house and any property he'd once owned.

Not only had he lost everything, but there was an official prejudice against him, making it almost impossible for him to get a decent job. Worse, the country itself was in tatters. Hồ Chí Minh's successors actually believed in socialism—they tried to make it work, and they collectivized the farms, created government-owned companies—cracked down on individual businesses—did all the things a Marxist government should do.

And all Communism did was bring misery to the people. They resorted to any work they could find, to buy food. Some wandered the jungles looking for dud 120mm rockets, and when they found them, dragged them back to the village, where they removed the explosives and cut up the aluminum to sell. Others worked in bicycle factories. Tân wasn't even allowed to do these simple jobs—not even the dangerous ones, like removing explosives from rockets.

But he survived.

He started anew. Later in life than most people, he married again, had a family, and encouraged his children to get a good education. Because it was difficult for him to find work, his wife started a small wholesaling business, buying ginger candy produced by nearby peasant women, packaging it, and then selling the product to retailers in Huế and Hồ Chí Minh City. And he was a strong part of that business, doing much of the work despite the physical infirmities caused by his imprisonment.

He thinks the Communists were bad people—but not Hồ Chí Minh. He thinks the Americans had the right idea, but didn't know how to go about helping Vietnam. Today he lives in a decent house and has two motorbikes, and his wife runs a prosperous business. He is proud of his children. At the time of the interview, he was sixty-three years old—and still had a child in school.

He doesn't live in the past.

And he doesn't hate anybody.

But all need to heal. The older Vietnamese I know have healed within the context of their culture. When I asked Thuy Sullivan why her father, Mr. Bang, did not suffer from PTSD after he had been left for dead in Quảng Trị in 1972, she smiled.

"Doug—have you ever looked at those men you see drinking beer in the afternoon and evening—the ones at a *bia hoi*[20]—the ones you think should be home with their families?"

"Yeah—I just figured they were a bunch of lazy drunks."

"Well then—what do you think about the clusters of men you see down by the river in the morning—the ones drinking coffee?"

"I don't know, Thuy—I never really thought much about them. They're just old men, I guess."

And Thuy went on to explain how the culture of building deep relationships in Việt Nam has helped people recover from the profound tragedies of war. Most of these groups of men have known each other since childhood. The women build similar groups in the markets. In both genders, these are groups of total trust. You can literally say anything within these groups—with the knowledge that you will be respected and loved by people you have known all your life. If one former soldier within your group wants to talk about the firefight where he was so scared he peed his pants, he can say it. If another says it was his fault that his squad leader was killed, he can say it. If a third recalls how he rummaged through the pockets of a dead enemy, and cried when he saw photos of the dead man's wife and children, he can say it.

"In other words, Thuy—the Vietnamese do as a regular part of their culture what Americans pay one hundred and fifty dollars an hour for on a shrink's couch?"

I was to have Thuy's opinion backed up when talking to a Vietnamese psychiatrist who had studied in Australia, and who had worked with Australian PTSD victims. Dr. Cat affirmed what I already knew—very few Vietnamese of the war generation suffer mental illness as a result of the war.

For Americans, healing may have to come in a different way.

Wards Five and Six at the 24th Evacuation Hospital—the Vegetable Garden—were tough places for a young nurse, but like her male colleagues serving out in the field, Cindy did her job as best she could. Sometimes she didn't think it was enough.

Some of the wounded on her ward were paralyzed. They required respirators—big machines that made the chest expand and contract in order to breathe. In 1969, the technology was such that respirators were too big to put on an airplane with a patient. The paralyzed wounded had to stay on Ward Five until they recovered enough to be able to breathe on their own and be sent back to the United States for further treatment. They lay on their beds—special beds that could be rotated so they didn't get bed sores. The medical staff put them all in the same area within easy hearing range of the nurses' station, and their breathing was constantly checked.

The danger in such treatment was that patients usually developed pneumonia, the result of never breathing deeply. Without occasional deep breaths, the lungs slowly filled with fluid, making breathing all that much

---

20 Bia hoi (say bee-ah hoy) – a small beer joint, often outdoors, where an inexpensive beer is drunk. The beer is made under a process shown the Vietnamese by the Czechs. It is brewed to be drunk within a few days.

harder. As more fluid accumulated, the harder it was for the soldier to breathe. Slowly—over a period of days or even weeks—some of the paralyzed became less able to talk. Rather than being able to yell out, "Hey nurse—I need my bed turned!" their requests became feeble, and soon became just grunts. Eventually, even a grunting sound was impossible, and they had to resort to making a clucking sound with their tongues.

Cluck cluck. Meaning, "I need my bed turned. Or at least come over to my bed and ask what I need; then I can shake my head until you say the right word."

Then one night, a corpsman or nurse would check on the young man, or someone would notice that he was no longer making clucking sounds. His family would next see him in full dress uniform at the hometown funeral home.

It wasn't that Cindy didn't do enough for the dying in any medical sense—it was that she felt she didn't do enough to ease their dying. The wounded knew—and she knew—that they were going to die. Despite the fact that hospice service for the dying did not exist in 1969, Cindy kept that emotional scar deep within herself, never letting it bubble to the surface.

Not until Christopher Reeve was thrown from his horse and paralyzed, needing a respirator to breathe and stay alive. Technology gave Superman a chance to live that Cindy's patients had not had, and the scar in her soul edged toward the surface. There it stayed for a while, occasionally prompting unpleasant emotions, but not ready for healing yet, either.

Healing came while on China Beach near Đa Nẵng in 2002. Each morning, the team members on the two-week medical trip organized by Vets With A Mission would meet on the beach for a short prayer and worship service, before going to the medical clinics to work in the slums.

One morning toward the end of the trip, leader Chuck Ward told us we were going to do things a little differently that day. Our group was made up of veterans and non-veterans alike. He said, " When we think of veterans, we usually think of men. But not all Vietnam vets are men—some are women. Our own Cindy Young is one of those—she served as a nurse during the war. And, like many of the men she cared for, she has her own demons from the war."

Chuck went on to say that he had never talked with Cindy about her experiences in the war, nor had they ever discussed any emotional wounds she might have had—Chuck only knew that the Holy Spirit had led him to believe that there was something deep down inside her that needed healing.

Then he asked Cindy to come sit in the chair next to him. She looked at me as if to say she had no idea what it was about, and I nodded for her to go—even as I whispered that I had never talked to Chuck about her experiences. Looking uncomfortable, she sat—then Chuck asked for all the guys in the group who had Purple Hearts to come forward. (I think I caught Chuck off guard when I came forward—he didn't know I had been wounded.) Joined by a helicopter pilot and another grunt from the 1st Cav, we stood behind Cindy, and then put our hands on her shoulders as Chuck prayed for her release—her healing—from whatever pain she had from the war.

Cindy faced her emotions—as difficult as they were to face—and when public acknowledgment came that she had indeed faced extremely difficult times during her service, the scar was brought to the surface, where it was healed.

Three Purple Heart recipients stood behind Chuck Ward as he laid hands on Cindy for healing.

Photographer Unknown

Healing is what allows Americans and Vietnamese alike to move on with their lives. Healing is one of the reasons older Vietnamese don't hate us—they have healed. Their lives look toward the future rather than dwelling on the past.

Though most veterans I talk to are astounded that I lived in Việt Nam, a surprising number of veterans visit the country. Cu was great at separating them from the rest of the tourist crowd, and calling me if he found someone he thought I'd like to meet.

I met Tom Murray on his very first trip back. We met Tom, a big burly guy with a deep laugh and rapid speech, along with his wife on one of the first days of their trip. Tom was still in "returning vet mode," and was trying to find all his old memories. Having been an artillery forward observer with an infantry company of the 1st Cavalry Division, he was brought out of the field when he was promoted to Captain. Flying out of the airfield at Phu Bai, he directed the big guns along the DMZ from a diminutive single-engine aircraft, and was shot down three times—once while over Laos. After his year and a half in Vietnam, Tom went home, coached high school football, worked with at-risk kids in schools, and went on to earn his doctorate.

Dr. Murray is not a typical college professor. He's more of a hands-on kind of person than a tweed-jacketed scholar. His return from Việt Nam in 2005 to his faculty position showed it. Full of energy, he started thinking about his students and how he could involve them in the new Việt Nam he was witnessing.

By June, 2006, he had succeeded. Four students from the College of Charleston arrived in Huế, where I hooked them up with six Vietnamese students.

Tom and I took them to Cu's Mandarin Café for dinner, where they could meet each other. After much giggling and laughter, as the Vietnamese students tried to teach the Americans how to eat with chopsticks, Tom and I gave them their briefing: "You guys are on your own for a few days before we start working at the orphanage. Don't try to drink beer like the Vietnamese—and whatever you do, let the Vietnamese drive the motorbikes!"

My instructions to the Vietnamese students were a little different: "Don't take your new American friends to tourist places—they can go to the kings' tombs and the Citadel without your help. Show them the real Hué. Take them to your villages—have them eat the same food you eat—show them a typical day in the life of a Vietnamese student."

And off they went, in a cloud of motorbike smoke. We learned they went swimming in the river near Vi's village. (Say *Vee*—she is at the far right in the photo of the students.) They went to pagodas and markets. They took the Americans far away from the tourist haunts, where students their own age hung out and families lived.

And it had an impact. Liz came back Hué to teach (and as of this writing is in Đa Nẵng), while Mike came back before going to grad school, and helped build a schoolhouse and library in the A Lưới (say *ah louie*) district—the area known to American soldiers as the A Shau Valley. Two of the Vietnamese students have studied in America.

Hate us? The young generation seems to be doing much better than their elders.

Three students from the College of Charleston and three from Đại Học Huế, at the end of their time together.

Many of my generation seem to cling to the past, whether they had seen service in the Vietnam War or not. Such a person is Peter Yarrow, famous as the Peter of the Peter, Paul and Mary folk music group of the 1960s. In 2005, Yarrow visited Việt Nam, and gave a free concert in Hà Nội.

And it was during that concert that he said, "On behalf of the American people, I apologize for what America did to your country."

Not an untypical thing to say, if you were someone who had never been to Việt Nam or Vietnam.

When Yarrow came to Huế for a concert (not a free concert either), Julie went with some of her Vietnamese friends. Because I wanted her reaction to whatever the aging folk star said, her post-concert comment was, "Doug—you're right. He is still living in the sixties."

Peter Yarrow just assumed that the Vietnamese must hate us, and would demand an apology. His contrition was based on the concept that America was all bad while the Vietnamese were all innocent. Whether Yarrow merely had an overly simplistic viewpoint or suffered from plain intellectual laziness made no difference—his apology was spoken to an audience who had moved on. The Vietnamese are far more interested in lowering the rate of inflation, bettering their education, buying a car, and increasing trade with America.

Though my students knew every Beatles song by heart—and they love the Carpenters—none of them had ever heard of Peter Yarrow.

And they didn't care either.

And they most assuredly don't hate us.

Father and daughter pray to their ancestors in a small pagoda north of Hué. The red ao dai on the man indicates he is a person of some importance in the village.

I bought into it. I really did.

Worse—I didn't know I'd bought into it.

Let me tell you how I came to a realization.

While living in Huế, I put some of my photos on the Internet—a photographers' site, not one for sharing snaps of family birthday parties. As I was wandering around some of the galleries by other shooters, I found one by an excellent photographer named Richard, who had begun his career in 1969 while in Vietnam. He has some wonderful black and white shots of his time in the war. The man had a great eye.

I wandered further around the site—and found more shots of present day Việt Nam by other artists. On one photo, Richard had commented that the shot was great, but went on to say that it looked like things hadn't changed much in Việt Nam in the past thirty-five years.

Richard was flat wrong about that! "Oh—you are wrong!" I thought. "Việt Nam has changed greatly, and is continuing to change. Please, Richard—come back to Việt Nam, bring your cameras and your considerable skills, and take another look. Việt Nam has changed."

And that's when I came to realize that I was guilty of perpetuating the myth that Việt Nam has not changed. I have been posting the cliché pictures on my blog—the ones folks back in North America expected to see. The exotic. The different. The picturesque. The slightly strange.

I had been posting pictures on my blog of little old ladies wearing conical hats. Shots of xích lô drivers. Tourist pix of The Citadel. Vietnamese food. Girls in ào dài. There are stories about schools for street kids, riding motorbikes, duck-herders, or hard-working and diligent students.

All of this is good—but it also did not represent all of Việt Nam.

Previous pages:

In the early days of Communist rule, everything pertaining to the old monarchy was anathema. Things are much more relaxed today. The Ngọ Môn Gate is a major tourist attraction, but it was once the place where the emperor entered the Imperial City.

Someone forgot to tell the young man on the right to wear sandals or other footwear suitable for an imperial guard of two centuries ago. His tennis shoes give away that this photo is of a present day event—a re-enactment of a traditional festival where the king asks heaven to bless the labors of his people.

The country is changing rapidly. Very rapidly. It has the second fastest growing economy in the world. It is not a "backwards" country; it is a developing country. Obviously, there are lots of little old ladies wearing conical hats. Equally so, there is much evidence of massive change in Việt Nam. That change is personified by the motorbike.

Getting around a Vietnamese town conjures up touristy visions of xích lô drivers and rickety bicycles. But in the emerging Việt Nam, the xích lô is going the way of the oxcart, and the bicycle has been overwhelmed by the motorbike.

Horse and buggy, little boys and mud puddles, shot and a beer, bread and butter, Red Sox, and Fenway Park…motorbikes and Việt Nam.

The motorbike is the family mover, and is used for runs to the market. In the two large cities of Sài Gòn and Hà Nội, it is in the early stages of being replaced by the automobile.

The old Honda Cub started it all, decades ago. These little 50cc machines are built like rocks—they don't break or even seem to wear out. The idea of the motorbike is to provide cheap, dependable transportation that is very easy to maintain. The Honda Cub exudes those qualities. You don't need much more than a screwdriver and a crescent wrench to fix a Cub. Honda still sells them, but it's rare to see new ones. Poorer people, particularly farmers, usually own them, and use them to haul all kinds of goods to and from market. The mufflers are loud, the gears whine, and they ain't pretty—but they work as hard as their owners.

By definition, a motorbike is not a motorcycle. A motorbike has a single cylinder, small engine size (under 150cc), and is meant to lug two people short distances at city speeds. On a good day, a motorbike maxes out at 60 kilometers an hour (about 37 miles per hour).

Rush hour in Huế brings out throngs of bikes such as these, seen crossing the very narrow bicycle/motorbike lanes of the railroad bridge.

Sophisticated urbanites want to make good use of time by multi-tasking, and that includes the Vietnamese couple on the go. Cell phone usage while driving is very common, as is texting. (Scary, eh?) Wondering about the face mask? Many ladies wear a mask while on a motorbike, to ward off the air pollution. The air in Sài Gòn and Hà Nội is bad, but it's merely an annoyance in Huế—at least for now. The couple is riding a Honda Wave, a much more recent model with an engine twice the size of the Cub, and with much sleeker styling. You can tell this one is not the newest model, because it does not have front disk brakes.

Following page: A motorbike can be more than just transportation—it can also be a statement. For this bright young college graduate, her motorbike says something about her. It is stylish, and is red to say she wants to be known in the world, and that she will someday ride a nicer motorbike—or own a car. Like other members of her generation, she is eager to get on with life. A motorbike gives her freedom to move about, and that newly found freedom of movement for young people opens them up to new ideas and ambitions.

As the economy improves and people's income levels have risen, the motorbike has evolved. It is no longer unusual to see modern step-through models (what Americans call a scooter), making it easier on the ladies to get on—especially moms to be. They all have an automatic transmission and ample sealed storage space—even a way to lock your helmet when the scooter is parked. They are more expensive and drink more fuel, but they are popular.

The transition from the bicycle to the motorbike, then from the motorbike to more expensive step-through scooters, is all indicative of change. But the new freedom of movement also changes lifestyles. Young people are the driving force in today's Việt Nam—by sheer weight of numbers.

And that sheer weight of numbers means few people really know how to drive safely—most didn't have Dad to teach them to drive safely, because Dad has only owned a motorbike for a few years himself. My friend Cu is in his mid-sixties (my age), yet has only owned a motorbike for ten years—he is a new driver himself. A rapidly developing economy, combined with a very young population, makes it seem as though the streets are full of sixteen-year-olds.

The result is a horrendously high traffic fatality rate. In 2007, there were fifteen deaths per one hundred thousand population—about forty people died each day—and there is a good likelihood that the number was underreported. In an attempt to stem the number of deaths, the country enacted a helmet law in 2007.

In 2002, we noticed that many motorbikes were cheap Chinese rip-offs of Japanese brands. We would see "Hongda" on the side of a motorbike, painted in the exact colors of the original. These bikes were cheap to buy, but the buyer also got what he or she paid for—an unreliable piece of junk. As time passed and the economy grew, we noticed fewer of these knock-offs. The Japanese companies now build their bikes in Việt Nam. The Vietnamese government (like America's) requires 20 percent of the parts to be manufactured in-country, but the Hondas, Suzukis, and Yamahas are all well made.

And it was my motorbike that led to my introduction to the Vietnamese medical system.

By the spring of 2006, I was totally at home on the chaotic streets of Huế, but my old body was not always able to do what I wanted it to do. As I turned right off the main street onto a side street, the usual pack of bicycles and motorbikes on the wrong side of the street approached. No big deal about that—just slow down some, and let them squeeze by.

Except that I was going too slow, and I lost my balance. As my motorbike fell to the street, the foot peg pinned my ankle bone to the curb.

No pain—nothing more than hurt pride. I assured the young people who stopped to help me that I was okay, hopped back on my motorbike. and rode off to go home.

Free valet parking for motorbikes at a club in Huế. More disposable income allows young people to indulge in club-hopping as well as to buy a more upscale set of wheels.

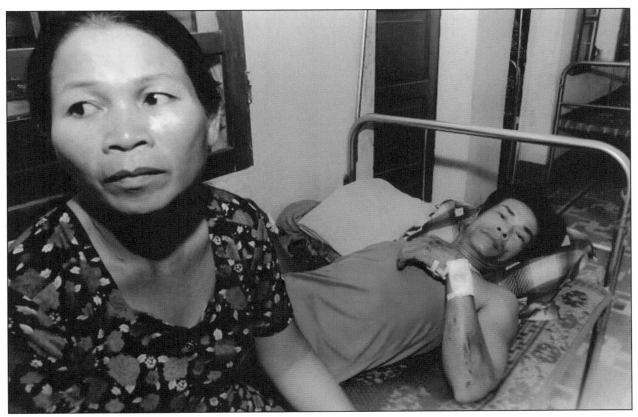

Though her husband is not seriously hurt, the woman knows he will not be able to work for awhile. The crush of traffic patterns, combined with a cultural tolerance for men riding drunk, leads to a very high incidence of crashes.

That night, the ankle began to throb. It was painful to walk on that foot. Cindy became suspicious that there was something wrong. The following morning, Cu went with us to the hospital.[21] X-rays were taken, the orthopedic surgeon in Huế talked to a Western doctor in Hà Nội, and a diagnosis was made.

I had a hairline fracture in my ankle. No walking on it for two weeks, and a cast was put on. It wasn't a bad break—it's what I called an old man's break. If I had been younger and my bones more resilient, I would have been fine.

Hospitals in Việt Nam work differently than they do in America. Need some medication? The doctor will tell you what the patient needs, and a family member will go to a pharmacy and bring it back to the nurse to be administered. Hungry? It is the family's job to bring food in for the patient.[22]

I didn't have to stay overnight. After my cast was put on, I was free to return to our apartment, where I was doted on by my wife. Over my protestations that he had a business to run, Mr. Cu personally brought me food from his restaurant—and stayed to chat.

21 Besides translating for us, Cu also made sure that the hospital knew we lived in Huế, as opposed to being merely tourists in Huế. That saved us a lot of money.
22 These things are changing rapidly. There is now a small cafeteria at the Huế hospital, and in some cases, hospital food is prepared for patients by the hospital staff. Families still must buy many medicines at pharmacies, but major drugs are now supplied by the hospital.

Of course people ride a motorbike in the rain. In Huế, the rainy season is from November through February. You wear rubber sandals because leather shoes will rot, and you learn not to mind the bottom of your pants getting wet.

This man is wearing a poncho, as most people do. It is normally carried folded up and tucked under the seat. Notice the clear place over the motorbike's headlight—the poncho was made specifically for using while riding a moto.

Cindy, too, had her experience with the medical system. One night, after returning from a good meal at a European restaurant, she suddenly collapsed—and screamed.

Loud screams. The kind of screams you hear in horror movies.

Though the very intense pain went away quickly, she continued to have a monster headache, and she was still in pain the next day. A call was made to a Western doctor in Hồ Chí Minh City, who advised she go to the Huế Hospital for an MRI. While she lay there in the Emergency Room, waiting for instructions from the staff, I looked around that dingy room and I decided I didn't want to have my first heart attack in Việt Nam.

Cindy lay on a gurney—I had to bring a blanket for her, as there were no sheets. The floor was plain concrete, yucky and grungy, with the occasional bloody bandage lying about. Cindy didn't have her glasses on—she couldn't see the big patches of green mold on the walls, nor the peeling paint. I watched as the victim of

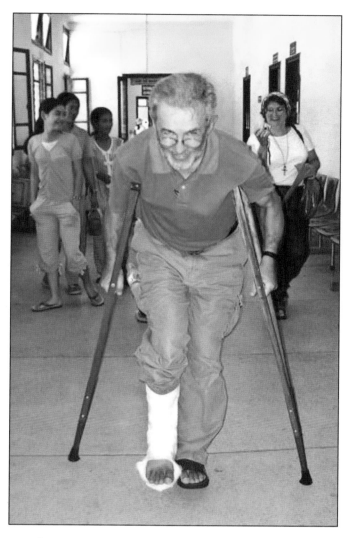

Much to the amusement of my wife and Mr. Cu, my Vietnamese crutches were a little too short for me.

Photo courtesy Phan Cu

the motorbike accident came in—head bloody, and in obvious deep pain. The family pushed his gurney into the room, where he was ignored.

This was third-world medicine.

The Vietnamese radiologist who read the MRI couldn't find anything wrong. After conferring with the Western physician, the decision was made to send her to Bangkok for a full work-up.[23]

Cindy recovered from her headaches in a week, and the crack in my ankle healed well enough to walk on after a month, but it took me much longer to get over what I saw as bad medicine.

It took two or three years to realize that Việt Nam's medical practices are in transition too.

Mrs. Cindy the English teacher is a Registered Nurse, having started her career as an Army nurse in Vietnam. At Cu's Mandarin Café during the spring of 2006, we met La Relle Catherman, another RN and the co-founder of MEDRIX. La Relle had a problem—the nurse who had taught MEDRIX's English Medical Terminology course to the doctors and nurses at the hospital could no longer teach it, due to the failing health of her physician husband.

Could Cindy teach that course that semester?

Of course she could—and wanted to do it. Her first class consisted of physicians who had won a grant to study in Australia—but they had to pass an English proficiency test first. There is nothing that pleases a perfectionist teacher more than a group of highly motivated students—and they were motivated.

That one course, taught while we still lived in Huế, blossomed into a calling. Since then, we have returned on an annual basis so Cindy can teach that course in the spring—she loves it.

And returning each year, we saw great progress at Huế Hospital, both in the physical plant and in the qualifications of the doctors, nurses and technicians. We saw a new building for pediatrics—a cardiac care department where bypass surgery and transplants were done—a new emergency room, replete with state-

---

23 Though we never learned for sure, the physicians at the big Bumrungrad Hospital in Bangkok strongly suspected that Cindy got a megadose of MSG in the salad she ate that night at the restaurant, and had a reaction to it. She has never had any recurring symptoms. My ankle, however, never returned to normal—to this day, it is still a little puffy.

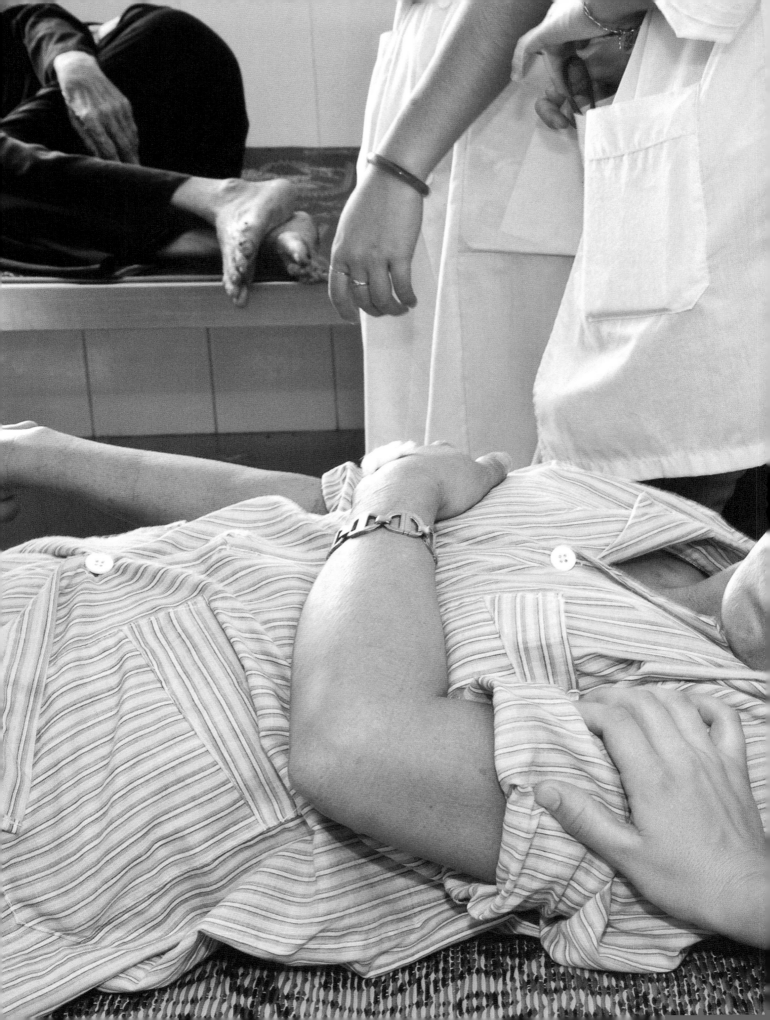

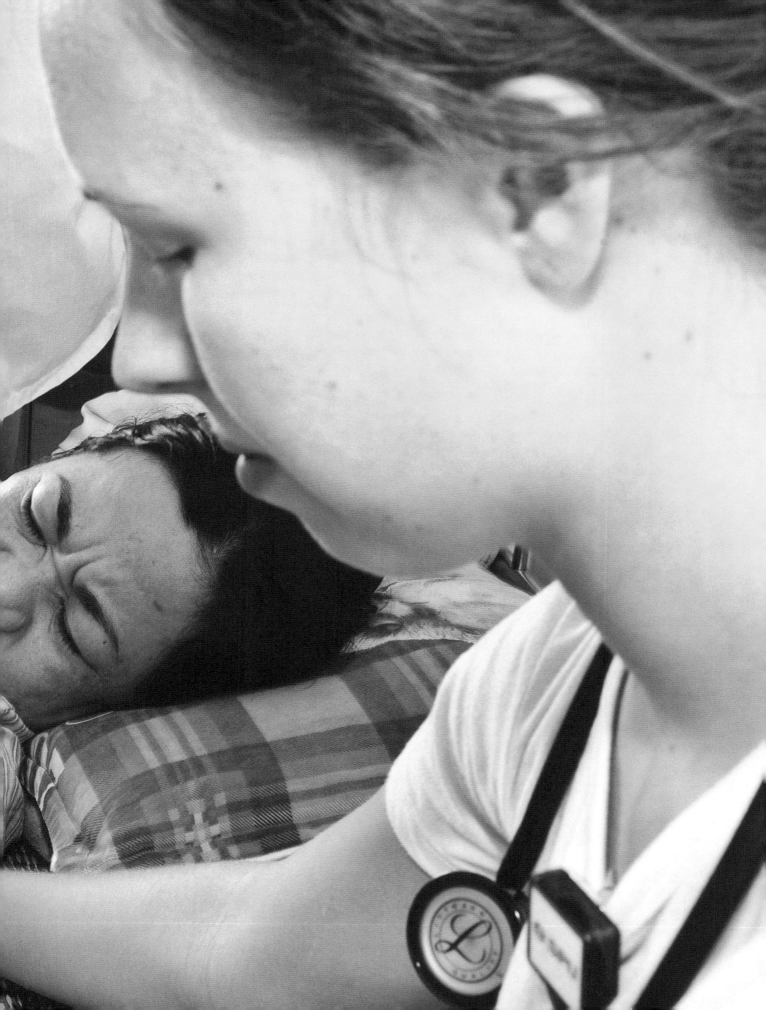

Previous pages: A student nurse from Seattle-Pacific University comforts and prays for a patient undergoing a painful procedure in a hospital in the mountain area west of Huế. The student nurses are learning under the direction and supervision of Vietnamese physicians, as part of their college studies. That is a role reversal—most Americans would expect us to be teaching the Vietnamese.

The program also matches American nursing students with Vietnamese students under the auspices of MEDRIX, a Seattle-based organization that has been operating in central Viet Nam since the mid 1990s.

We met the founders of MEDRIX while still living in Huế. La Relle and Bob Catherman put both Cindy and me to work after we went back to the U.S. to live. During many return trips, Cindy has taught an English Medical Terminology course to physicians and nurses at the Huế Hospital, and I've been involved in safe water projects.

Another victim of a motorbike accident is transported from the Huế Hospital Emergency Room to his ward. Japan has donated a lot of money to build the Huế Hospital into a modern regional medical center, complete with a cardiac surgery department that does heart bypass surgery on a regular basis— even heart transplants have been done there. It is another example of the very rapid change of the country. Both the United States and Australia have training programs at home and in Việt Nam to upgrade physician skills.

of-the-art ambulances. We saw a new ophthalmology building erected—and it included lecture rooms with modern multimedia capabilities. We saw a dilapidated regional hospital in the mountainous area west of Huế rebuilt into a modern facility that would be the envy of any rural hospital in America.

As for my having my first heart attack in Việt Nam? Not a problem now—and I wouldn't even have to leave Huế to get first rate care.[24]

Prior to moving to Huế to live, we had taken photos during our trips to Việt Nam. We took photos in Đà Lạt, in Hội An, Hồ Chí Minh City, Tây Ninh, Quy Nhơn, and in small towns. Like most Western tourists, we were fascinated by the open markets. Anyone who travels to Asia is obligated to take market photos— you know the photos—the ones with the smiling old lady and some sort of exotic foods or freshly slaughtered animals on display—ones seen earlier in this book.

If it's important for you to take pictures of exotic Vietnamese open-air markets, you'd better call a travel agency and book your flight soon. In the cities, huge supermarkets like the Big C are cropping up quickly. In a few more years, city dwellers will be shopping at the newer, more modern markets, and the open farmers' markets will exist only in the countryside where tour buses seldom go.

When we arrived in Huế in 2005, there was one small store that stocked Western food items. We went there for peanut butter, ketchup, and breakfast cereal. It wasn't much different from other stores—it opened out onto the street, had shelves floor to ceiling, and had glass show cases for the baked goods they sold. The clerks were tolerant of us, pointing to the goods we wanted. I never figured out if they took mercy on us and charged us the normal price, or if they gouged us. I prefer to think they took mercy us—they certainly saw us often enough.

By the fall of 2005, the first "supermarket" had opened. The Thuan Thanh market was three stories high and completely air-conditioned, and had scanners at the checkout counters. The bottom floor had groceries, the middle floor, clothing and non-food items, and the top floor, furniture and home furnishings. The grocery section had a nice produce area right near the refrigerated section. The frozen foods were at the end of the aisle. Most of the patrons were middle-class Vietnamese women. Again, none of the clerks spoke English, but I also could stroll the aisles, put my selections in the shopping cart, and then go to the checkout counter where the scanner tallied up my bill. No negotiating here—the price was on the can, just like home.

By 2009, there were three Thuan Thanh markets in Huế—each nicer and bigger than the previous. But they were all eclipsed in 2010 with the opening of a Big C supermarket, a huge place not unlike Wal-Mart.

Somehow, I don't think the average tourist wants to take a picture of a superstore.

Like most of the other changes taking place in Việt Nam, the growth of big supermarkets is being driven by the tidal wave of young people. They neither want to haggle over prices when they shop, nor do they care to get the latest news in the market—they can get that on the Internet, or via text from their friends.

---

24 To be impartial, there is still much that is wrong with the Vietnamese health care system. Despite being a Communist country, health care is not free. Health insurance is a new concept that few participate in. The practice of medicine is costly and that often means care is not rendered if money is not forthcoming. Rural health care is still spotty—many of the physicians in those clinics are there because they are required by the conditions of their education to serve in rural areas before they are allowed to practice in the cities, and they are not always happy about that.

Change is coming in other ways too—once atheistic Communist Việt Nam now has freedom of religion. The constitution was amended to mollify the Americans when diplomatic relations were restored between the two countries in 1995. While this change is not necessarily driven by the young, it is also true that many of the Christian churches have a goodly number of young people in attendance on Sunday mornings.

There is religious freedom in Việt Nam, but it is not the kind of freedom Americans enjoy. People can worship as they please—pagodas, churches and temples are open—but religious organizations must be approved and registered. Faith-based groups, whether Christian, Buddhist, Cao Đài[25] or others, are not allowed to own any public media—hence no religious newspapers or television stations. Churches are only allowed two days each year to invite non-members—and those dates must be cleared with the police. Home churches are technically legal, but must be approved like any other religious group— and they are seldom approved. Attending an unapproved church could put a person in jail. It is also illegal to evangelize—to spread religion.

Big C is a French company. Their huge stores have been in Hà Nội and Hồ Chí Minh City for years, but only recently have these multi-storied superstores come to Huế. You name it, you can buy it at a Big C. From frozen food to motorbikes to clothing to housewares, it's on one of the three floors. No bargaining skills needed—everything is barcoded and rung up at a cash register.

---

25 The Cao Đài faith was founded in Tây Ninh Province in 1926. It combines elements of Buddhism, Christianity, and ancestor worship with some unique ideas. It has between two and three million adherents.

A young woman, affluent enough to own an expensive step-through motor scooter, looks over a display of shoes while stopped at a traffic light. Her bare shoulders and colored hair are not traditional Việt Nam.

One of my students came to class one day dressed in a t-shirt emblazoned with "Florida Southern College, Lakeland." No big deal, except that the small liberal arts college is my alma mater. I asked her where she got it, and was told, "At a shop on Hùng Vương Street." (Say Hoom Voo-ung) She wasn't aware of and didn't care what the shirt said. She just cared that it was something in English from America.

Young people don't want to dress in traditional clothes, and they don't want to look like Mom and Dad. Fascinated by Western culture (I once saw a Britney Spears poster on the wall of a rural farm house), they are trying to find a balance between the traditional filial duties to respect their parents and trying to become more independent.

If you ask the average Vietnamese what his or her faith is, they will most likely say "Nothing" or "Buddhist." Technically, about eight percent of the population is Christian (and the vast majority of those are Roman Catholic), with a smattering of Cao Đài, but the large majority of Vietnamese practice something they don't refer to as "religion." It is ancestor worship, the veneration of previous generations who have become spirits.

Ancestor worship has blended well with Buddhism, and is central to the Vietnamese belief system. Generally speaking, Vietnamese believe that in death, one does not just cease to exist. Instead, one passes on to another world, which invisibly exists beside the world of the living. The dead people who are not worshipped become disturbed by the lack of attention, and prey on the living. The deceased who are pleased with the devotion paid to them can have a beneficial effect on their living relatives. Their supernatural powers can bring the living happiness, good luck, and even money.

Almost every home, especially in rural areas, has an altar, replete with photos of the deceased, incense holders, dishes for food offerings, and other paraphernalia. Outside the home is a small concrete (sometimes wooden) miniature "house" where the spirits dwell.[26]

The practice of ancestor worship made its personal impact on me in August, 2008, when I returned to Việt Nam to bring Phan Thuy Trang to America to begin her graduate work. In the days before her departure, there was to be a big party—a goodbye party in her honor.

It seemed as though the entire village was there—old folks, kids running around—and lots of women cooking food. As I rode into the home's courtyard, it was obvious that everything was ready, but the festivities hadn't begun.

The ancestors needed to be told that Trang was leaving with a white man from America—and that it was okay for her to leave with him. She had her parents' blessing, and now her father, grandfather, and her grandfather's brother all put on their áo dài, lit incense, and asked the ancestors' blessing on her travels. Prayers were said before the family altar as well as in front of the spirit house. Once the food had been blessed, a portion of it was placed on the altar for the ancestors.

It will be interesting to see what happens to the regular practice of ancestor worship as Việt Nam changes. With its long history of being influenced by other cultures—including China (which occupied Việt Nam for nine hundred years), France (which colonized the country for one hundred years), and the United States (in the south for fifteen to twenty years)—Việt Nam has adapted itself and embraced some foreign practices, while often changing the new culture to suit itself. There is something about the Vietnamese, in that they always stubbornly stay Vietnamese.

Following pages: In the countryside near Huế is a small Catholic village. It obviously had a rough time after 1975, after the Communist take-over of the South. What was once a Catholic school is now abandoned and forlorn, a weather-worn cross still perched on top. Nearby is a partially constructed building that was probably meant to be a rectory. Both buildings were in semi-ruins.

Today the church building itself is in good repair—and the villagers practice their faith. On a Wednesday afternoon at five o'clock, the church bells rang and people gathered for prayer.

---

26 This may be a regional practice. I seldom saw a spirit house in Hà Nội, and never in Sài Gòn. Some of Huế's cultural practices are not practiced elsewhere. These are the little houses I saw outside people's homes on our first day in Huế, as we drove in from the airport.

The Buddha's Birthday is celebrated in Huế with a parade and many traditional religious practices.

My friend Thanh is praying for the spirits of those for whom nobody else prays—the lost souls. She is standing on the bridge over the Perfume River, where she had ritually thrown some food into the water.

Huế is a very conservative city in a country that is shaking off some of the traditional beliefs. Though described as a Buddhist country, the actual practices combine strong elements of ancestor worship with Buddhism. Thanh believes that if nobody prays for and cares for a soul, that person will become an evil ghost who will do damage to people.

Women are often the ones who do the daily work of leaving food for the ancestors and placing flowers on the altars, but older men have the family duties of honoring the family ancestors during Tết, the Vietnamese New Year.

Every home in rural central Việt Nam has a spirit house similar to this one, containing an incense holder and small vessels for food.

The older men of a household have the duty of performing ceremonies at Tết (Vietnamese lunar New Year) and other special times. They don formal áo dài (say owe yie), as the spirits might be offended by casual wear. Trang's father held three joss sticks (incense) for prayer, and prostrated himself three times. This family altar is fairly typical. Photos of the deceased are on display behind the altar, though in many instances, the photos are on top of the altar.

Note the men in the background watching, but Trang's sister barely pays attention to the ceremony. This is men's work, and she has kitchen duties.

155

Stubborn or not, the traditional is giving way to change. Better transportation means families can range further from home in search of work. Better communications allow those who live far away to stay in touch. Even in the small village where Trang's parents live, they have high speed DSL Internet connectivity.

Business is in the throes of change too. Easiest to see are the large multi-national companies such as Hyundai, Big C, and Mercedes. Starbucks has yet to arrive, but Pizza Hut is in Hồ Chí Minh City, Hà Nội and Biên Hòa. Ford has an assembly plant in Việt Nam, and Intel recently opened the largest computer chip fabrication plant in the world. Check out your Nike shoes—there is a strong likelihood they were made in Việt Nam.

But much of Việt Nam is still primarily a Mom & Pop small business country, where people live above their shop or next to it. The little shops are everywhere. While teaching a class, Cindy might text me and ask me to bring home something from the store—the proverbial quart of milk and loaf of bread. I'd stop by the little grocery store on a side street near Sư Phạm and get the bread and some Laughing Cow Cheese—the family knew me and always smiled, and we would exchange simple greetings.

And the stores are not restricted to just the main streets, as they are in America—they are also in the *kiệts* (say *kyets*) of Huế, the narrow alleyways where most of the population lives.

Just as with the stores, there is an army of craftsmen whose shops are part of their homes. The craftsmen make just about anything imaginable.

Phu is a metalsmith—a good one. His earthen-floor shop is next to his home on a kiệt in the old area of the city. It is difficult to tell which part of the building is home and which is shop. His small son has free run of the place, though to my eyes, there are many dangerous tools he could get in trouble with. The boy does well in school—in fact he is beginning to learn English. He greets me with a torrent of words as I enter the shop:

"Hallo! How are you? I am fine. What country are you from?"

"I am fine. You speak very good English. I am *mỹ*." (*Mỹ* is slang for American.)

"Thank you."

His English vocabulary exhausted, he runs off to get his father, who has been contracted to make the metal housing for a safe water device for MEDRIX. He has made a number of the housings—not only of high quality, but he made some dies that should allow for other people to replicate his work and increase production. Phu hopes that he can work with the provincial water authority to make these housings in large numbers. Today, he will be teaching other metal smiths how to make the housings. They will work for him in their shops, and his business will grow.

Americans usually stay away from alleys—that's where you can get hurt. In America, alleyways are dark and abandoned after work, but in Vietnamese cities, it is the alleyways where people live. This is where you will find families and babies and parties and pets. In Phu's kiệt, the men work on the metal in the shop—Phu's wife brings them food and beer—the men take a break for a cigarette—neighbors drop by for a chat—and the little boy plays with his friends.

Get over your fear of narrow alleys, and walk down a kiệt in Huế.[27] It's where you will see the real Việt Nam.

---

27 Alleys are called kiệt in Huế, but *hem* in Sài Gòn and *ngo* in Hà Nội.

A cold rainy day in winter. The center of this kiệt has concrete blocks that can be removed. Under the blocks are the sewer and water pipes of the city. There are no zoning laws, as there are in America. Along this kiệt are beautiful new homes with air conditioning and modern furniture, as well as some very run-down old buildings.

The men leave their shoes at the door, and then break out the bottle for a party. Though I was invited to join them, I demurred and met the old man whose self-appointed task it was to watch and tally the neighborhood goings-on.

Far from being dangerous, these alleys are where the lifeblood of Việt Nam flows. As the economy grows, more people become members of the middle class—and more people leave these tightly knit communities and build plush new homes in the outskirts of Huế.

And the emerging middle class builds homes both akin to, and yet unlike, their American suburban counterparts.

The lots are tiny; therefore, most new homes are more vertical than single storied, and homes are built very close to one another. Note the garage, now housing bicycles and motorbikes, but there is obvious hope for an automobile in the future. The driveway spills out onto a street—not a narrow kiệt.

The new middle-class homes have multiple bedrooms, an indication that children will have their own rooms rather than having to share space with siblings. In most cases, the entire house is not air-conditioned—electricity is still too expensive for that—but the master bedroom is usually cooled, and often the main living area is as well.

This house is in the Vỹ Dạ (say *Vee Yah*) ward of the city. When we moved into our apartment in the guest house in Vỹ Dạ in September, 2005, the surrounding area was rice fields.

Today, the rice fields are gone, and Vỹ Dạ is the bustling new place to build homes for affluent middle-class families. Nice homes have sprouted, as have chic restaurants and comfortable coffee houses. The kiệts may be the place to find the "real Viet Nam," but Vỹ Dạ is the place to find the emerging Việt Nam.

But the Vietnamese have a knack for continuing to be Vietnamese. With money to spend, they could opt to build houses you might see in Indianapolis or Seattle, but they keep their own perspective on things. The houses are distinctly Vietnamese, and so are the coffee houses.

There are no Starbucks in Việt Nam—and I'm not sure Starbucks could flourish in a place with so many distinctive and excellent coffee houses. These are the places where the young elite gather, to talk about their new smart phones, to swap stories about their plans, and to continue in the Vietnamese tradition of friends seeing each other frequently.

Ái Nhân (say *Eye Nyun*) is another of my former students. I think she has been in every coffee house in Huế, because she takes me to a new one on every return trip. Some are built with the old hardwood beams used for mandarins' houses, now torn down. An enterprising merchant purchased much of the scrap teak and ironwood, stored it, and waited for the price to rise. Many of the finer restaurants and coffee houses in Huế are now "beam houses"—luxury establishments built with the old wood.

If you are not a coffee drinker—too bad. Việt Nam is not only the world's second biggest exporter of coffee, but Vietnamese coffee is excellent. (Saturday morning is *Trung Nguyên* time at our house in Texas—Trung Nguyên being a brand of Vietnamese coffee.) If you want something else, the coffee houses offer a huge variety of teas and health drinks.

I'll never understand the economics of the Vietnamese coffee house. You are invited to come and sit and dawdle with friends—you are not rushed—yet with the low table turnover, the price of coffee in these places is very low. Good coffee—better friends—and cheap.

If you are a returning veteran who was once stationed in the I Corps area, there is a good chance you went through the big base at Phu Bai. For the Air Force, it was the farthest north of all their bases, and there were major Army and Marines units there as well.

The Vietnamese aren't wasteful—here was a perfectly good airstrip, so they turned it into the commercial airport for Huế. Tens of thousands of tourists come into Phú Bài each year, with multiple daily flights from both Hà Nội and Hồ Chí Minh City on modern Airbus 320 or 321 aircraft.

No, you won't see anything to do with the war at Phú Bài either. Mr. Cu once drove a fire truck at the airfield for the Americans—his fire station is long gone.

Automobiles are not unusual sights in Huế, though the streets are not clogged with them—yet. The vast majority of them are Japanese brands one might see anywhere in the world. Many auto makers, such as Toyota, Mercedes, and Ford have large assembly plants in the country. If you visit Việt Nam using a tour agency, most likely you will travel in comfort in an air-conditioned van. Even if you decide to "rough it" and travel by bus from city to city, you will ride in a modern Korean-made vehicle. The day of the colorful, smoke-belching, overloaded local bus is just about gone.

The next time you see the exotic photo of the Vietnamese pedicab known as the xích lô (sometimes referred to as a cyclo), just remember that the real Việt Nam may be a bit different than expected. The real Việt Nam may be driving a Ford.

Lest I be accused of sounding like a shill for Việt Nam, there are some serious shortcomings.

And the biggest shortcoming is corruption.

Communism as an operative form of government is dead. Việt Nam is no more "Communist" than Mexico is Buddhist. The Communism as preached by Lenin is supposed to provide free education and medical care to everyone—the state should own all businesses—and food should be provided by big collective farms. After Hồ Chí Minh died in 1969, his successors actually believed in socialism. When the country was reunified in 1975, the ideologues who took over the country almost sent it into bankruptcy.

Though some large companies are still owned by the government, most have been sold off to private investors or have become publicly held firms. There are two stock markets in the country.

But the fly in the pie is corruption. When the Communist Party instituted Đổi Mới (say *doy moy*, meaning renovation) in 1988, it began the process of changing to a "socialist-oriented free market economy." (If you can figure out that oxymoron, you are smarter than me.) It quickly devolved into a system of thinly disguised bribery. If you wanted to start a business—cross somebody's palm. We know of one woman, educated at the Teacher's College at the University of Huế, who taught at a remote mountain village after college. When she married, it cost her and her new husband five thousand dollars to bribe the right officials so she could get a teaching job in her home village.

At the first Communist Party Congress following the war in 1976, the Number One item on the agenda was corruption.

At the Communist Party Congress concluded in 2011, the Number One item on the agenda was corruption.

Of course, none of this has much effect on the average Westerner visiting, or on those living in Việt Nam, but if the country is ever to take its place as an economic power like South Korea or Taiwan, it will have to solve this most basic of problems.

The old and the new stand side by side in Việt Nam. It is a country in transition—no longer a poor country—it is now a developing country. The surge of young people continues to transform society, despite some efforts by the government to control things. Though Facebook is blocked, you would never know it, because the young people quickly figured out ways to go around the blockage.

Tourists arriving in Huế will fly into Phú Bài Airport, about twenty miles south of the city. The bottom floor is where you will find the ticketing desks. Once having passed through security screening, passengers go upstairs to the departure lounge. Though new, the airport is not the most modern, but then again, it is a smaller regional field compared to the much larger airports at Hà Nội and Hồ Chí Minh City.

Most Internet usage takes place in Internet cafés, but that too is changing, as the economy grows and more people can afford to buy their own computers and use them at home. When we first arrived in Huế, our Internet connection was dial-up on a very flaky 14.4 kbs system. When we left, we were using a DSL connection.

Bob Dylan himself said it—the times, they are a-changing. It is not your veteran's Việt Nam anymore. It is changing as fast as it can figure out how to change.

Cu and I were photographing a local village celebration of the old men in a pagoda, but the young man was intrigued by me. Out came the smart phone, and he had some pictures of the old Westerner with the huge camera to show his buddies. Grandpa went back to drinking rice wine with his buddies.

DEROS

DEROS—everyone who served in Vietnam knew what their DEROS was.

Date Estimated Return from Over Seas—the date you could go home from Vietnam. We soldiers made it a word—we referred to our "*Dee* Rose." (Rhymes with gross.) The day when we would go back to The World. The day we would be "Leaving on a Jet Plane." The day when we would leave The Nam. We created "short-timer calendars," and if we had less than one hundred days to go, gave ourselves names like "Two Digit Midget." Or we'd say, "I'm so short, I could sit on a dime and swing my legs." On the day we left our unit..."I'm not short—I'm next."

We couldn't wait to get the hell out of Vietnam!

Cindy and I both left Vietnam in March, 1970, she about two weeks before me. My battalion was at LZ Andy when I left. The bittersweetness of leaving is something difficult for civilians to understand. Of course I very much wanted to get away from the war and from Vietnam, but I also felt like I was deserting my men.

John Orr drove me to the airfield in an open jeep, both of us in jungle fatigue uniforms covered with the red dirt of Quan Loi. John and I had become friends after I left the field and became the battalion adjutant. (Personnel and administrative staff officer.) He was drafted into the Army after he ran out of money to stay in law school. In combat, his company commander had sent him to the rear area after John earned his third Purple Heart—and he became my legal clerk. We'd gotten drunk together a few times, and the night before I left the 1st Cav, we got drunk again. He'd been a good friend, though he was hardly a model soldier. He did his job, but the military life was not for him.

We waited next to the runway until the C-130 landed. After it blew more red dust on us, we both got out of the jeep. I reached into the back of the vehicle for my duffel bag. Hoisting it on my shoulder, I glanced at John.

Specialist John Orr was at a rigid position of attention. With the deliberateness that comes from deep feeling, he snapped off a precision salute that was beyond the criticism of any drill sergeant. No words—only a salute.

Preceding pages: Trang had been an undergraduate honors student in the American Culture course I taught during our first semester. The following fall, she asked me to be the faculty advisor for her fourth-year honors research thesis. After finishing second in her class, she moved to Hồ Chí Minh City to work for IBM as a procurement specialist. In 2008, she came to the United States to earn her Master's degree. Following graduation, she was hired by the university as a lecturer. During the three years she lived near us, Trang became very close—the daughter we never knew we needed.

Never have I returned a salute with greater military decorum. I held my return slightly longer than necessary, and then slowly lowered my hand. He waited until my hand was at my side, finished the salute, climbed into the jeep, and drove off.

That was probably my last truly military act. From there, I was on the way home and out of the Army

Every Vietnamese or Filipino band that played in the military clubs in Vietnam knew the song, "We Gotta Get Out of this Place." I listened to it one last time at the Officer's Club at the 90th Replacement Battalion. Along with the rest of that crowd who were going home, I came drunkenly to my feet to sing the chorus, while the FNGs ("Funny" New Guys) shrank into the corner, wondering what in the hell lay ahead of them.

But I couldn't get too drunk—I had to be sober enough to hear the announcement that my bus was leaving to go to Bien Hoa Air Base where I would get on "The Freedom Bird."

And like every other soldier who got on that airplane, I sure as hell never expected to return to Vietnam.

Incense in the making. To the southwest of Huế, on the road to many of the emperors' tombs, is a village where the making of incense is the mainstay of the economy. The early morning sun struck the sticks as they were drying, while Cindy and I were out on one of the thoughtful motorbike jaunts we made just prior to leaving Việt Nam.

Of course, I did return to Việt Nam—but in June, 2006, it was time for us to leave again. Our feelings could not have been more different from those in 1970. Though I had not been able to learn the language, I was now very much at home in Việt Nam. I had friends—Vietnamese friends—whom I would miss greatly.

As the time for departure grew nearer, we became more aware of what we would miss. Some days, we just hopped on the motorbike and putted around town—I knew my way around Huế better than I knew my way around McAllen, Texas. We wanted to ride around and soak everything in—wondering if we would ever smell *nước mắm* (fish sauce) again, see joss sticks burning in front of homes again, hear the little jingle played by the popcorn carts on the streets at night again, or see the lights on the Trương Tiền Bridge again.

And we ate like we were never going to eat Vietnamese food again—*bánh ướt* at the Huyền Anh restaurant in the Kim Long area of Huế—*phở* at Phở Sài Gòn—*banh khoái* at the little joint near the market off Bến Nghé Street—or *bún thịt nướng* at Phương Nam, our favorite lunch place.

Cindy and Trang enjoyed a late afternoon talk on Vọng Cảnh Hill, overlooking the Perfume River west of Huế.

In between our giving final exams, taking melancholy motorbike jaunts around the city, and eating at all our favorite haunts, Trang and Tuan came over to our apartment to help pack. We'd come to Việt Nam with two duffle bags each. A year and half later, we were having a large crate built to ship all our "stuff" back by boat. Trang helped Cindy carefully wrap some of the delicate items we had accumulated—the Vietnamese are great gift-givers, and we had acquired carved xích lôs, beautiful cups, exquisite statues, framed embroideries, scale model hill tribe long houses, and lots of other reminders of Việt Nam that now cheerfully clutter our home in Texas.

And, as is the Vietnamese way, all our friends wanted to be the last person to say goodbye. The last few days were filled to exhaustion with coffee house meetings, farewell dinners, visitors at the apartment, gifts brought (though we had finished packing the crate), and lots of phone calls.

Damn, it was hard to leave.

But we knew it was time. Family duties beckoned.

I had become a little bit Vietnamese, and I knew it was time for me, as the first son, to take care of my mother. Simple forgetfulness had morphed into a diagnosis of Alzheimer's. It became obvious to my siblings that Mom would not be able to live by herself in her home in Florida much longer. Mom needed to be near family—and because the rest of the family lived in cold weather climes, she needed to be with us in south Texas.

Leaving Việt Nam was not like leaving Vietnam. Times had changed—rather than getting on a stretch DC7 at Bien Hoa Air Base for the trip back to "The World," in 2006, we boarded our Japan Airlines 767 at Tân Sơn Nhất Airport for the six-hour flight to Tokyo. (In 2007, a new international terminal was opened. It is as modern as any in the world.) Back in 1970, we had no passports. In 2006, we had our passports checked and stamped. We waited for our flight in a comfortable air-conditioned lounge, not a steaming hot room with benches. Thirty-six hours after Cu took us to the Phú Bài airport, we were back in Texas.

There is culture shock—and there is also reverse culture shock. Some experts will say reverse culture shock can be worse than the original.

But we didn't have time to indulge in reverse culture shock. We didn't even have time to retrieve the crate of personal property we had shipped from Huế—it hadn't arrived in Houston yet. Our first task after returning home was to move Mom from Florida to south Texas, where she would live in semi-independence a few houses away from ours.

Strangely, the incident that ended her independent living was also associated with Việt Nam. In January, 2007, I made the first return trip to see Cu, who was quite ill. On my return home, Mom and Cindy were going to meet me at the airport, but when I got off the plane, no Mom and no Cindy.

Cindy's brother Mark said they were at the hospital emergency room.

Walking across the airport parking lot, Mom had fallen, breaking her hip. The surgery and anesthesia were too much for her withered brain to handle, and at the age of ninety-one, she was in a nursing home for the remainder of her life. I made a daily trip to see her—to talk with her—to hold her hand—to be her son, even when the day came when she no longer knew who I was.

Those daily trips were hard. The woman who had once done the New York Times crossword puzzle with an ink pen could no longer remember her own name.

Besides caring for Mom, I was going through "Việt Nam Withdrawal."

Bob Catherman had emailed me from Huế that Cu was not doing well. He was so ill, he did not come to the Mandarin Café to greet tourists and sell them photos—he just stayed at home in bed, with a very serious case of depression.

My long flight back to Việt Nam in January, 2007, was longer than normal—not because it took more hours, but because I kept wondering if I had waited too long to come back, or had failed Cu in some way. You know how people blame themselves for things they didn't do.

The long flight ended, and after checking into a cheap hotel, I rented my old motorbike from Huy and went to see my friend. Lying on his bed, barely able to say hello to me, was the guy who normally sprang from his chair at the mere sight of a tourist at the entrance to his café. This was not my old friend Cu curled up in the bed. He ate little, drank some tea, and barely reacted when his grandson Ken came into the room.

I sat by his bedside for hours each day. Often he would drift off into sleep, but I was glad I was there when he woke up. When he was awake, he didn't talk much. I didn't know if it was better when he was awake or asleep. When he was awake, he just stared at the ceiling. I brought a book with me to read while he slept, but I soon realized I wasn't reading—I was just staring at the pages.

In Việt Nam, the making of a friend is serious. One doesn't meet someone at a party, then go to the office the next day and refer to that person as "my friend." Friends are like family. Friends are important.

Cu didn't talk to just anybody about his war experiences—he only talked about his war experiences with friends. During the first year I lived in Huế, Cu didn't talk to me about the 1968 Tet Offensive, nor did he discuss the trauma of getting his wife back to Huế for the birth of their first child in May, 1975, just days after the fall of the south. Cu would share his horror stories about the war only with friends.

Cu and I had slowly become friends.

And as I was sitting there watching him during his illness, I didn't like what I saw on my friend's face.

I'd seen vacant expressions like Cu's on men's faces before. During the time I commanded Charlie Company in 1969, we had ten men die in combat. (I don't know how many were wounded during those months—my guess would be thirty to forty.) I'd seen troopers who had been in one too many firefights, or who'd seen a buddy killed or badly wounded. After the men in the squad divided up the canteens and gear they wanted, some guys went into a funk. Carrying a friend's body bag to a waiting helicopter tends to make you think you won't go home yourself. It's not that they had given up—they just felt like their time in hell would never end. Cu seemed that way—like he couldn't see the end of his troubles.

Slowly, over the space of weeks, Cu began to respond. I desperately wanted him to go see Dr. Cat, the head of the Department of Psychiatry at Huế Central Hospital, but he resisted.

"Cu," I said, "I really want you to see Bác Sĩ Cat. Please."

After a few moments of uncomfortable silence, I tried again, using guilt as a weapon.

"Cu—I came from the other side of the world to see you. The least you can do is humor me and go see Bác Sĩ Cat."

He'd drift off back to sleep, and I would wait in the chair next to his bed. I fought off my own funk as I watched him.

As I sat there, I remembered an afternoon when I was living in Huế. After teaching a class, I'd gone by the Mandarin Café for an iced coffee. The place wasn't busy, so Cu and I sat down at a table overlooking the street. We sat there for forty-five minutes without speaking. It was a comfortable silence. We just watched the world go by and enjoyed each other's presence. *Già rôi* (*yah roy*)—too old. Two old men comfortable with being old—comfortable with each other.

Once again, I was reminded about the importance of relationships in Việt Nam. Because we were friends, Cu slowly began talking to me. Each day, my visit to his bedside would be a little longer. The day came when he walked outside the house with me.

Finally, he agreed to go see Dr. Cat.

The trip was good for Cu—and it was good for me. Without the demands of teaching, I had time to wander around Huế with my camera. It helped me get over "Việt Nam Withdrawal." By the end of my trip, Cu even felt well enough to join me, wandering the streets shooting night scenes.

But that first trip back to Việt Nam merely delayed my reverse culture shock. Funny thing about culture shock—I found out that those experts were right—reverse culture shock is worse. When Cindy and I arrived in Huế in 2005, it took us six to eight weeks to go through the stages of culture shock, but my adaptation to living back in my own country took much longer. I was a very angry (and very difficult to live with) person for the first few months.

> After living in a country where all media are controlled by the government, it was hard listening to people complain about problems, even though they never stopped to realize they had heard about the problems via a free press.

> After riding a motorbike because an automobile was way too expensive, it irritated me to read a bumper sticker on the back of a Hummer that read, "High gas prices suck."

> After living in a country of thin and fit people, it was baffling to see fat people circle their cars around store parking lots for a half hour just so they wouldn't have to walk very far.

> After living in a place where friends dawdled for hours over coffee, it was hard to watch people wolf down a burger, and then say, "I have to go—so many things to do." Of course, part of my irritation was

SAME RIVER, DIFFERENT WATER

the knowledge that the person in a hurry probably didn't really have anything important to do—she just had a *busy* thing to do. Our culture measures a person's worth by their busy-ness.

After living in a place where arguing with political leaders could land you in jail, it was hard to listen to people complain about their government—and tell you they don't vote, or they just don't care, or they are too busy watching *American Idol.*

After living in a country where people must get approval to invite newcomers to their churches, it was frustrating to hear my fellow Christians say they didn't invite anyone to church because "religion is a personal matter and I shouldn't impose my beliefs on anyone else."

Back on Page 88, there is an email sent to me by an anonymous student of mine. Compare her life as a student to American students' whining about how there isn't enough parking at school.

I had changed, but my home country had not. The crux of the problem was that my thoughts were about Việt Nam, but Americans still talked about Vietnam.

One email was from a young photographer telling me what great pictures I had taken while living in "The Nam."

Then there was the counselor who asked how I was doing after living in "The Nam."

The Nam? Both of these people weren't even a twinkle in Daddy's eye when the war was going on in Vietnam. Neither person was a veteran, yet they called the country "The Nam."

We veterans usually referred to the place as The Nam when we were there—it was the normal thing to say. "Hey man, when I get home from The Nam…," or after pissing off some higher ranking person, "What're they gonna do? Send me to The Nam?"

After asking both the photographer and the counselor to please refer to the country by its real name of Việt Nam, I went on to ask if they would like it if foreigners referred to their country as "Amerika" (Am muh *ree* ka).

Prior to 2002, I too might have used the term, "The Nam," but when I heard the words during the first veterans' reunion I attended after returning from living in Việt Nam, I heard them with fresh ears.

I heard "The Nam." I heard Vietnam referred to as a shit hole. I heard the old pidgin Vietnamese we used: "I dee deed over there as fast as I could," meaning you went someplace fast.[28]

"You number one GI"—American soldiers certainly heard that phrase a lot.

When I heard the word "gook," I thought of my former students, working their tails off to get an education. While not pleasant to hear, at least I could understand why veterans talk like that. It didn't offend me.

---

28 The Vietnamese word, *Đi*, means to move or travel from one place to another. American soldiers regularly used the word twice as an emphasis, along with the word *mau*, to tell villagers to move quickly. It became part of their own slang.

But why would young people use such language? I could only fathom that they were taught by their elders that Vietnam is a war.

As Trang pointed out to me once, "Thay—when I Google 'Việt Nam,' most of what I get is about the war."[29]

Just as I had learned to accept the fact that Asia was not going to change just because Doug Young had arrived, I now began to realize America wasn't going to change simply because Doug Young had lived in Việt Nam.

I began to mellow out.

But I also needed to keep a connection to Việt Nam, and I really wanted to work with those wonderful students I'd had. Cindy and I couldn't live in Việt Nam anymore, so we brought Việt Nam to us.

There are a lot of photographs in this book, but there is one missing. It's missing because it was never taken, though the image is burned into my memory—the image of Trang's face when she realized she would be able to fulfill her dream of studying for her Master's degree in the United States.

After a nice dinner in Sài Gòn, the three of us returned to our room at the Rex Hotel, where Cindy and I laid out the details. Most Vietnamese seem to think you either must get a scholarship to study in America or you must pay full tuition—which is impossibly expensive. Most Vietnamese I talked to did not know that a student can work as a graduate assistant, and not only earn money, but also qualify for much lower tuition.

When the details were all on the table, conversation ended and the silence became awkward. Trang examined her toes, eyes downward in thought. Finally Cindy broke the silence.

"Trang—is this really something you want to do?"

Trang now knew the dream was more than a dream—it could become real. It would mean living in a very strange place—she would have to speak English all the time—she would have to study and work harder than she had ever worked before—and she would be away from family. It was scary and exciting at the same time.

Very softly, she answered.

"Yes."

Hating to see that wonderful mind of hers go to waste, Cindy and I sponsored Trang (and later, Ái Nhân) to come to the United States for graduate work. While Trang had some idea of how much her life would change, Cindy and I had no idea that having Trang around would change our lives too. It tied us closer to Việt Nam, and we gained two daughters.

---

29 *Thay* (say *tay*) is the Vietnamese word for teacher. Trang and Ái Nhân insisted on using that title to address me after they came to America to study. I cannot imagine any higher honor than them calling me Thay.

Back in 1985, when my son was a college freshman, I took a business trip to a city near his campus. He drove down to meet me; we had dinner together, and then had a few beers in my hotel room as we caught up on each other's lives. Keith has a rather special link to the war—he was born in 1967 during my first tour.[30] The conversation drifted to the war.

"Dad—what would you have been like if you hadn't gone to Vietnam?"

On the face of it, the question seems rather silly—how can anyone know what they would have been like if they hadn't gone through a certain experience? But digging deeper, I realized it was a very good question.

And I couldn't answer him.

If my middle-aged son were to ask the question today, I would have to have him clarify the question—did he mean the first time, during the war, or the second time, when there was peace?

Though we never really know how much an experience changes us, it is certain that the war affected me. As years have passed, I think I can attribute some part of my personality to having been in combat—a certain impatience with those who dwell on seemingly unimportant things, for example.

I once held a job in which most of the senior managers were worriers. To my mind, they seemed worried about trivial matters. After one staff meeting where their pettiness had shown through, I was in the office of another gentleman who felt like I did. It turns out, he too had been in combat, though a different kind. He had been a Navy pilot who flew over Hanoi often. He described seeing enemy anti-aircraft missiles as they flew up toward his aircraft. Describing them as "flying telephone poles," he saw them shoot down a number of his friends, many of whom were killed. Having both been in combat, we agreed on this point—if you have been in combat, you seem to develop a knack for understanding what is important and what is not.

And we referred to this ability as "green tracer syndrome." In other words, if you see bullets come in your direction—bullets that glow green as opposed to the red bullets fired by American weapons—then you know someone is trying to kill you. That, we agreed, was important. Worrying about the color of your tie when the company president is coming to visit is not important.

Certainly, having been in a war in Vietnam changed me. Equally certainly, living in a peaceful Việt Nam changed me too.

I had learned a lot more about my own culture, simply because I had lived in another.

I remember how upset I had been at the Vietnamese seeming inability to plan. They couldn't even plan when an academic semester would begin or end. They couldn't plan on a way to repair the malfunctioning air conditioner in our room. My blood pressure soared, those first few months.

Until I realized that the Vietnamese have far fewer stress-related heart attacks than Americans do. I calmed down.

---

30 Keith was born to my first wife, Judy. He was six months old before I saw him.

Until I realized that traumatized Vietnamese war veterans were healed by the normal interactions of a culture that values community. They weren't left to flap in the wind like veterans in the American culture of individualism.

Until I realized the members of my generation of Americans can't get beyond the past, yet the people who live where the war was fought have moved on.

And, of course, I realized more than ever the value of relationships.

The new relationship I valued the most after we returned from Việt Nam was the one I had with Trang. Yes—of course—she is a very bright woman and an excellent scholar, and she does more work by accident than I do on purpose. She dug into her studies with dedication and hard work. She worked for the university as a graduate assistant—another twenty hours a week on top of her studies and classes.

We knew we could not provide a Vietnamese community for Trang, to help her adjust to life in America. We'd had a small group of Americans who lived in Huế, and they were a great help in our assimilation. When Trang arrived in America, Cindy decided that she wanted our home to be a place for Trang to restore herself after a long week of studying—a place to call home. Weekend visits from Trang were treasured, whether we just watched old movies on the tube, or enjoyed long discussions late into the night.

The Vietnamese have a saying—if someone teaches you half a word, that person is your teacher for life. Trang calls me Thay (say *tay*), which means teacher. But the truth is, Trang is also my teacher. She taught me something more about relationships.

Mom had been in a nursing home for over six months when Trang arrived. My daily visits were difficult for me—this was, after all, my mother. I certainly didn't expect anyone else to visit Mom.

But Trang would sometimes ask to go see her.

Why in the world would someone—particularly a young person—want to go visit an old person with advanced dementia?

Because I had lived in Việt Nam, I knew the answer. In traditional Vietnamese homes, it is not unusual for four generations to live together. Rather than the mantra spoken by American retirees who say, "I don't want to be a burden to my children," the Vietnamese consider it to be the normal way of doing things—the children and grandchildren are expected to care for Mom and Dad. Trang had cared for her grandmother in the last part of her life. Being around the elderly was not something that spooked Trang. She's not like American kids who are only around old people when they visit Grandma at Christmas time. American kids certainly don't see Grandma when she is dying.

If I were in a traditional Vietnamese family, I would not have been caring for my mother—my grandchildren would have been caring for her. Mom would have been a normal part of life from the time they were born.

My mother died of complications from Alzheimer's at the age of ninety-three. Trang often joined me on my visits, seemingly enjoying her time with Mom.

I am not naive enough to believe that's how things are still done in Việt Nam. In their fierce desire to become a "developed" country, the Vietnamese are quickly divesting themselves of many old ways of doing things. The extended family is no longer as central to their culture as it used to be, as the children, especially educated children, leave the nest to pursue their future in the big cities. Mom, Dad, Grandma—and maybe even Great Grandpa— remain in the village.

Of course, not everything that works well in Việt Nam works well in America. We are a people who prize our independence—a characteristic my mother took to her grave, saying she didn't want to bother her children. We are a nation of self-reliant people who model themselves after the cowboy. Remember chaotic traffic? In Việt Nam, it is everybody's responsibility to be sure not to hit anyone in front of them. That could not work in America—our spirit-of-independence philosophy tells us we are very important, so we drive too fast, and honk our horns in anger as we demand others place us ahead of them.

But just as I got used to living in Việt Nam, I slowly learned to live in my native America again. I find myself back to scheduling my days, and I seldom meet anyone for coffee. Where once I would spend an entire day out in the countryside with Cu, taking photos, I have returned to the normal American life of knowing many people but having very few true friends.

Reflections – An Epilogue

Why Việt Nam? I'm not positive, but I think it has something to do with the soul being fed. Living in Việt Nam required energy. It was both difficult and satisfying at the same time. In my life experience, I do my best when I am a little uncomfortable. Yet there is a peace over me in Việt Nam that exists nowhere else. I am convinced God owns a condo on the barrier island east of Huế—a place where He can watch the sun come up out of the ocean in blazing glory each morning, then after a busy day taking care of the world, watch the sun set behind the mountains while He sips a Huda beer.

The journey for Cindy and me is not over—it probably never will be. Though we don't make regular trips back to Việt Nam anymore, and though there are still Vietnamese students here in America whom we love as this is being written, I know that one day they will move on, and there will be no Vietnamese young people in my life. I will miss them greatly.

It can be reasonably argued that Việt Nam was the biggest single factor of my adult life—my son was born while I was there—I met my wife there—I bought my first serious camera there, and was reintroduced to photography there—and I met young people there who became the excitement of my dotage. Being in Việt Nam during both war and peace provided a sense of purpose and duty that I have experienced at no other times in my life. I experienced the worst of times and the best of times in that country.

Does my positive experience with modern day Việt Nam somehow diminish my experiences in combat? Does the loss of the lives of the ten men who died while I commanded C 2/5—and the men from my platoon in the 199th who died—make no difference anymore?

Most certainly not. In 2011, I photographed a story for a newspaper about a large "Welcome Home, Vietnam Veterans" celebration. The place was thronged. Part of the exhibit was "The Wall That Heals," a half-sized replica of The Wall in Washington. I knew I could get a nice photograph there, so when I saw a man in a wheelchair, I moved closer and took a few shots as he pointed to names on the wall. I quietly asked him when he had been in Vietnam, and in what unit. He looked up at me, but his speech was too slow and too slurred. Taken aback, I looked at his wife and adult son, but they could only tell me he was there in 1966—they didn't know enough "military speak" to know the unit.

Then I spotted the miniature Combat Medic Badge on his ball cap. Having seen my own medics perform heroics that defied belief, I somehow knew the man had been out front, caring for a wounded grunt, when he himself was shot.

Shot in the back. Paralyzed. In a wheel chair.

And I lost it. I was not the epitome of a photojournalist, but I muttered something to the family about medics, as I tried to choke back tears. When I failed, I walked away, fighting for composure. It was an unexpected reminder that I do indeed love modern Việt Nam, but the memories of war are still deep inside.

I still can't bring myself to visit the long-term wards at a Veterans Administration Hospital—I'm afraid of what I might see. Also, we're not all heroes—my being wounded does not mean I was a hero. The Army awarded me a Purple Heart even though I had screwed up—I wasn't supposed to get shot—I zigged when I should have zagged. The heroes are those who earned their Purple Hearts and still battle the aftereffects all these many years hence.

Strangely, I feel I have come full circle on the issue of talking about my experiences in Việt Nam.

Like most veterans, I didn't talk to many people about my experiences in the war, and I still don't. Those who had never experienced war would sometimes say (behind our backs, of course), "Oh goodness! See what Vietnam did to him. It was so terrible, he just can't talk about it."

And that is unmitigated silliness. If you have ever been to a reunion of Vietnam veterans, you will find most of them can't shut up—they talk nonstop about the war.

They just don't talk about war with someone who has never been in combat.

I once had a heated discussion with my sister Karen. When I returned from the war in 1970, I lived with her and her family for a short time. Many years later, while we were on a ski trip, it rained. Skiing in the rain is no fun, so we went into Salt Lake City to a movie—"Forrest Gump." The movie has some heavy-duty combat scenes in it, and as I watched, I realized I was sucking air through my teeth. Cindy reached over and took my hand, and I knew I would be okay.

But later, my sister was upset with me.

Karen: "You lived with me for four months when you came back—and you never ONCE talked to me about Vietnam.

Me: "True—I never did. Karen, how many kids do you have?"

Karen: (With a puzzled look on her face) "I have two—you know that."

Me: "Then why the hell didn't you ever talk to me about childbirth?"

The lightbulb came on. Just as she would never discuss having babies with me—a man—neither would I discuss combat with her—a person who would have no idea what I was be talking about if I told her that " *Alphabet's M-60 jammed when we made that CA into Rita and his sector of fire was filled with gooks in a bunker. An RPD opened up out of that bunker, and I had to low crawl over toward 2-6 until the fast movers put some snake and nape on the tree line.*"

Sorry, Karen—I joined the exclusive "Vietnam Veterans Club" a long time ago. We talk differently than you do. We see the world differently than you do. You can't join our club.

Our experiences and our language even keep family members out of our club.

Mrs. Jankovich knew her son as "Billy," but to his buddies in his squad, he was known as "Alphabet." In Hawaii, Mrs. Takahashi called her son Jason, but out in the jungle, he was known as "Pineapple." Alphabet was a machine gunner, and Pineapple his assistant. They depended on each other for their very lives—literally.

Pineapple did not come home from Vietnam to go into Mom's kitchen, eat the favorite foods Mom lovingly cooked just for him, and then tell Mom how Alphabet got hit by a rocket propelled grenade, splattering brains all over the trees. Pineapple doesn't tell his girlfriend what a dead NVA soldier smells like after three days in the tropical heat. Pineapple became Jason again, and kept quiet about what it was like to dig a hole in the ground every night—and how he laid out his weapon, magazines, Claymore detonator, and grenades in front of his hole in anticipation of an attack.

Separated from those who knew what we had experienced, and surrounded by well-intentioned but unknowing people, we veterans just kept quiet. Jason's mom and his girlfriend may have wanted him to open up and talk about Vietnam, but they don't belong to The Club.

Today, of course, I don't have horrible stories to relate to my American friends. Rather, I have lots of fun stories to tell—stories of exotic foods, wonderful students, fabulous photographic experiences, and all the other good times I had in Việt Nam. But the separation between their world and the world I know in Việt Nam is too great, and few of my friends want to hear about it. As Yogi Berra once said, it's déjà vu all over again.

And so I am now—I have experienced both Vietnam and Việt Nam—combat and peace. Though I much prefer the peaceful Việt Nam, few other people, except those who have also lived there, want to talk to me about it.

As a practicing, believing Christian, I have read many times that "God works in mysterious ways." While I believe that with all my heart, I also prefer to express that in the vernacular.

God is weird.

I return to a place where I almost died—in fact, I almost died numerous times—yet nowhere else on earth is there a place where I feel as alive as in Việt Nam.

Now I know Việt Nam is a country, not a war.

I know the war is over, though I know this is not the last time I will have that thought.

Thanx, God—I am blessed.

Tạm biệt Việt Nam

Good-bye, Việt Nam

Made in the USA
Charleston, SC
21 February 2013